VISIONS OF THE OTTOMAN EMPIRE

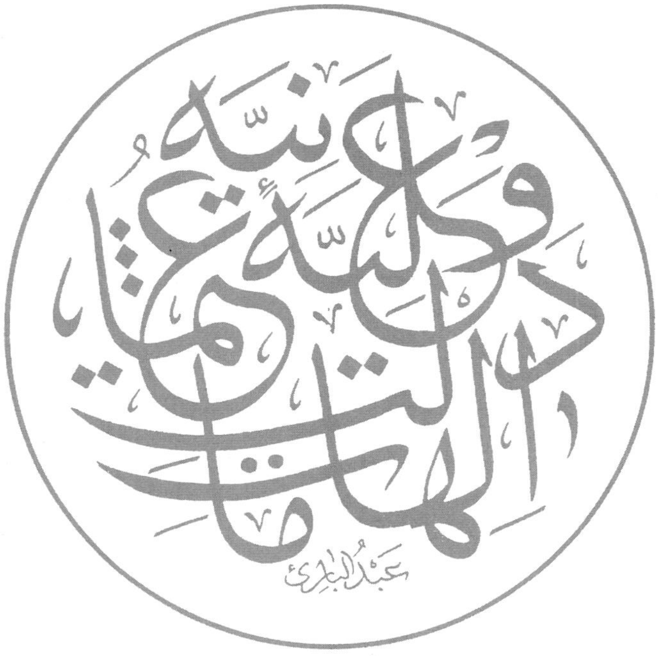

VISIONS OF THE OTTOMAN EMPIRE

SCOTTISH NATIONAL PORTRAIT GALLERY
EDINBURGH · 1994

Published by the Trustees
of the National Galleries of Scotland
for the exhibition held at the
Scottish National Portrait Gallery, Edinburgh
16 August – 6 November 1994

ISBN 0 903598 49 3

Designed and typeset by Dalrymple
in Adobe Minion and FontFont Humanist
Printed by BAS Printers Ltd, Over Wallop

Cover illustration: John Frederick Lewis
Indoor Gossip, Cairo: a Scene in the Harem 1873
(Whitworth Art Gallery, Manchester)
Traditional Turkish marbled paper
from Mitchell & Malik

Facing title page: calligraphy by Talip Mert
Visions of the Sublime Ottoman State

In this publication a modified transcription system has been used which will allow the English reader to come as close as possible to the original Ottoman or Arabic pronunciation without the use of diacritical marks.
The captions and texts in quotation remain in their original forms.

Foreword

The pursuit of the 'Orient' has played a leading role in western culture, ranging from the fantasy of the tales of the Arabian Nights to the physical reality of the Bible Lands. The civilisations which comprised the places and people of the Ottoman Empire were geographically, historically and ethnically so extraordinary and so diverse that they acted both as a magnet and as a light to the West. Artists seeking freedom from the constraints and limitations of their own society found in the Near East a source of vibrant inspiration which revitalised western culture. Romantics of the nineteenth century like Lord Byron and Eugène Delacroix invented an Orient of the mind which was filled with drama and exotic colour. Travellers and Arabist scholars like Robert Hay or Edward William Lane found an equal fascination in the reality and opened the eyes of the West to the complexity and richness of the countries and peoples of the Empire. Painters who visited the Near East, such as Sir David Wilkie, David Roberts, John Frederick Lewis and William Holman Hunt explored the visual range of that complexity. And when, in the 1840s and 1850s, photographers like Félix Teynard and Auguste Salzmann followed, they found themselves compelled by the land and the architecture to adopt what now seems a surprising modernity of vision. The reality that they saw caused them to shift their art, like a mirage, from its formal western foundations.

Such are the themes and concerns of this publication and of the exhibition at the Scottish National Portrait Gallery. The exhibition has been made possible by the generosity of collectors, curators and scholars worldwide. We owe a particular debt to the staff of the Musée d'Orsay, and especially to the late Philippe Néagu, for giving us early encouragement by so generously agreeing to lend a large group of their magnificent photographs. We are also profoundly indebted to Michel Laclotte, Director-General of the Louvre, for enabling us to borrow a number of highly important works that will grace the exhibition.

In addition we would like to record a sincere debt of gratitude to the following: Professor Gerald Ackerman; David Alston of Sheffield City Art Gallery; Janet Backhouse and Shelley Jones of the British Library; Professor Yehoshua Ben-Arieh of the Hebrew University of Jerusalem; Frank Bicknell; Michael Borghi of Borghi and Co, New York; Madame Thérèse Burollet of the Musée du Petit Palais, Paris; Madame Françoise Cachin and Mlle Françoise Heilbrun of the Musée d'Orsay, Paris; David Bryden and Alison Morrison-Low of the National Museums of Scotland; Patsy Campbell; Alastair Cherry, Ann Matheson, Ian Brown and Richard Ovenden of the National Library of Scotland; Simon Edsor and Andrew McIntosh Patrick of the Fine Art Society; Lindsay Errington of Aberdeen

Art Gallery; Jane Farrington and Stephen Wildman of Birmingham Museums and Art Gallery; Helen Guiterman; Ian Jones, photographer; Vivien Knight of the Guildhall Art Gallery; Susan Lambert, Mark Haworth-Booth, Charles Newton and Janet Skidmore of the Victoria and Albert Museum; Briony Llewellyn; Christopher Lloyd, Surveyor of The Queen's Pictures; Patricia MacDonald; Neil MacGregor and Nicholas Penny of the National Gallery, London; John Murray; Mr and Mrs Michael Price; Dr Roberto and Mrs Lillian Hay Regano of Milan; Duncan Robinson of the Yale Center for British Art; Pamela Roberts of the Royal Photographic Society, Bath; Nicholas Serota, Director of the Tate Gallery, London; Charles Saumarez Smith and K. K. Yung of the National Portrait Gallery, London; David Scrace of the Fitzwilliam Museum, Cambridge; Colin Simpson of the Williamson Art Gallery and Museum, Birkenhead; Alastair Smith of the Whitworth Art Gallery, University of Manchester; Joanna Soden of the Royal Scottish Academy; Hugh Stevenson, Glasgow Museums and Art Galleries; Roger Taylor and Paul Goodman of the National Museum of Photography, Film and Television, Bradford; Ann Thomson; the Reverend Leslie Selwyn Tillett; the Right Honourable the Earl of Wemyss and March; Professor Christopher White and Catherine Whistler of the Ashmolean Museum, University of Oxford; Stephen Whittle of the Harris Museum and Art Gallery, Preston; Mr F. E. B. Witts; Andrew Wyld of Thomas Agnew and Sons.

The curator of the exhibition, Julie Lawson, would also like to thank all those friends and colleagues who have given invaluable advice and support: Janis Adams, who saw the publication through the press; Estelle Barr; Alison Boocock; Anne Buddle, Registrar of the National Galleries; Chris Claxton; Robert Dalrymple, who designed the publication; John Dick, Keeper of Conservation in the National Galleries and his colleagues John Watson, James Berry and Graeme Gollan; Christopher and Elizabeth Ferrard; Zoë Hall, who designed the exhibition; Heinz and Bridget Henisch; Valerie Hunter; Victoria Keller; James Lawson, who shared insights and eased domestic burdens; Stephen Lloyd; Margaret Mackay; Julia Rolfe; Liz Smith; Sara Stevenson; Helen Watson.

We must also acknowledge generous support for the exhibition from the following: Blackwall Green (Jewellery and Fine Art) Ltd; The Hope Scott Trust; Messrs Martin and Frost; Momart Ltd; and the Trustees of the Stanhope Palmer Charity.

TIMOTHY CLIFFORD
Director, National Galleries of Scotland

DUNCAN THOMSON
Keeper, Scottish National Portrait Gallery

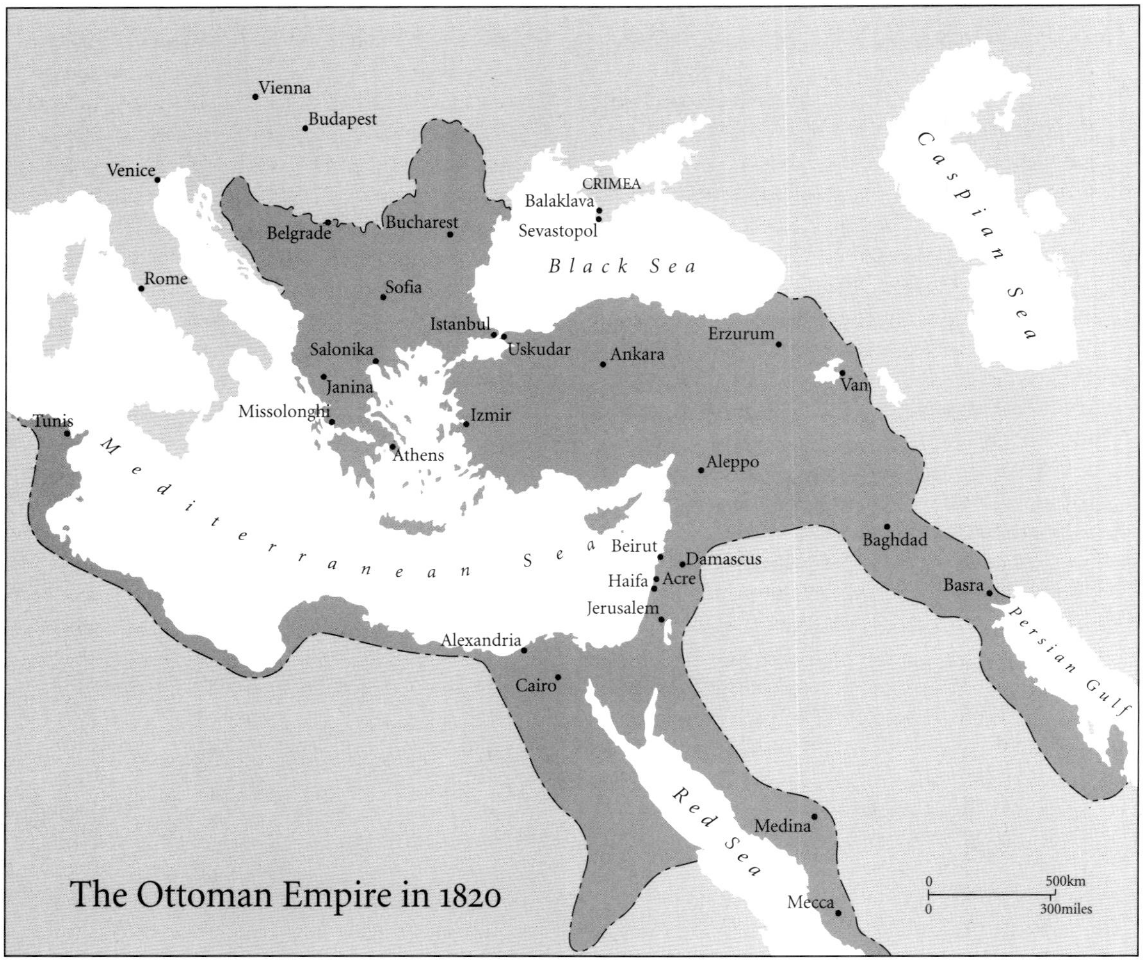

The Ottoman Empire in 1820

The Sublime State

Christopher Ferrard

THE Ottoman Empire in the seventeenth century may have been a place of mystery for the Westerner, but for the Ottoman subject it was a place of certainty. This certainty manifested itself in the attitude of Ottoman subjects to the Ottoman State and their attitude to the outside world. The Ottoman establishment was Muslim and subscribed to a system of thought that was founded on the precept that Truth could be based only on the revealed word of God, ultimately to be found in the Holy Koran. The Ottoman State was an Islamic state in which a great part, and at times the majority, of the population was non-Muslim. The challenge of incorporating and successfully subjugating so many non-Muslims was met in a particularly Ottoman way, partly an adoption of Islamic models and partly a uniquely Ottoman innovation whereby the non-Muslims were organised into three subject nations. The three nations, based on religious rather than ethnic identity, were the Orthodox, the Armenians, and the Jews. Each of these nations was given autonomy in matters of religion and civil law. The Muslim establishment took little interest in the internal organisation or intellectual life of the non-Muslim nations. The Ottomans did not even have a concept of empire, one nation subjugating others, but rather of a single state in which many nations lived with privileges and duties accorded to the Muslim 'nation'. The Ottomans referred to their state as *Devlet-i Âliye* (The Sublime State).

The Ottoman establishment was traditionally divided into two social categories: the Men of the Sword and the Men of the Pen. The former category encompassed the military and governmental personnel, who conducted the secular affairs of the state while the latter comprised the legal and teaching professions. The secular arm of the state was staffed entirely by Christian-born converts who were all slaves or manumitted slaves of the sultan. Taken from the Christian population of the Balkans at a young age, these slaves were trained to become either Janissary troops, the crack infantry of the Ottoman Empire, or servants in the palace. The brightest among them were destined for higher positions and were given a thorough training in the skills necessary for administration. As the slaves had converted to Islam, their sons were brought up as Muslims and were therefore ineligible for service in the secular arm of government. The professions available to them were scholarship and the law. Thus the sons of beys and pashas could become effendis but never beys and pashas themselves. Thus was created a state in which political power was held entirely by one man, the reigning sultan. There was no Ottoman aristocracy comparable to that in Western Europe, a situation which attracted the admiration of Machiavelli when he was formulating the political bases of the ideal state, about the year 1513:

The Turkish empire is ruled by one man; all others are his servants ... It is difficult to win control of the Turkish empire but, once it has been conquered, it can be held with ease ... The reasons for it being difficult to succeed in winning possession of the Turkish empire are that there is no chance of being called in by the local princes ... And this is because of the reasons I gave above: they are all slaves bound in loyalty to their master...[1]

In the reign of Suleyman the Magnificent (1520–66) the Ottoman Empire underwent a major reorganisation in its administrative and legal systems. This codification of the law was to earn Suleyman the title of *Kanuni* (the Lawgiver), the name by which he is known in Turkey. Within this codification all aspects of life were regulated, even the garments that the various members of society were to wear. These regulations were to be in force for the next 250 years. Successive generations were to look back to Suleyman's reign as a golden age and indeed there was a great deal of justification in this view as the Empire was at the apogee of its power and the state institutions were seen to be working well. The most celebrated western traveller of this period was Ogier de Busbecq, the ambassador of the Holy

Roman Emperor to Suleyman. He was struck by the good order that prevailed throughout the Ottoman dominions. Writing in 1555, he describes the Sultan's army which was on campaign to Persia:

Now come with me and cast your eye over the immense crowd of turbaned heads, wrapped in countless folds of whitest silk, and bright raiment of every kind and hue, and everywhere the brilliance of gold, silver, purple, silk and satin.... A more beautiful spectacle was never presented to my gaze. Yet amid all this luxury there was a great simplicity and economy.[2]

Busbecq was also immensely impressed by the social structure of the army and government:

Those who hold the highest posts under the Sultan are very often the sons of shepherds and herdsmen, and, so far from being ashamed of their birth, they make it a subject of boasting... Thus among the Turks dignities, offices and administrative posts are the rewards of ability and merit; those who are dishonest, lazy and slothful never attain to distinction, but remain in obscurity and contempt. This is why the Turks succeed in all they attempt and are a dominating race and daily extend the bounds of their rule. Our method is very different; there is no room for merit, but everything depends on birth; considerations of which alone open the way to high official position.[3]

Had he but known it, Busbecq was witnessing the final days of the Ottoman golden age, for the seeds of corruption and decay had already been planted and had taken root. The Ottomans themselves were the first to be aware of the corruption that was permeating the State at all levels. For two centuries the state institutions continued to decay from within, while the frontiers of the Empire were being constantly eroded. A number of Ottomans wrote memoranda to the reigning sultans documenting the evidence of decline and suggesting remedies. These remedies were invariably the implementation of the laws as codified by Suleyman. The State was weak and degenerate because the rulers had strayed from the old ways.

The fundamental conservatism of this great Islamic state could not give regard to anything that was taking place outwith its territories. There were cultural and other ties with the Islamic states to the east but when it came to the Christian world to the north and west there was nothing worth knowing, nothing worth learning. The Ottomans had insulated themselves from the western infidel and his world. The non-Muslims within the Empire, however, posed no threat and were treated with benign contempt. They wore oriental garb and were an intrinsic part of the ethnic and religious patchwork that made up the complex social structure of the Empire. But the western (non-Ottoman) Christian was treated with complete disdain, for not only was he an infidel but he insisted on wearing infidel garb to prove it. All educated Ottomans would have known both Arabic and Persian but none in this period would have learned a Western European language; it was of absolutely no interest to him.

By the beginning of the eighteenth century the Ottoman establishment was becoming aware of the superiority of western technology and the question arose as to whether it was permitted for Muslims to adopt infidel inventions. The consensus was that they were acceptable in the defence of the Sublime State. In fact, from the outset there seems to have been little reluctance to adopt western military innovations and the Ottoman army adopted artillery and hand-guns at a very early date. In certain areas, such as naval and maritime affairs, the Ottomans gladly accepted western ideas, but these ideas were very much within maritime circles and did not affect general awareness. However, by the early eighteenth century the Ottomans had suffered two major reversals, the first at the Treaty of Carlowitz (1699) the other at the Treaty of Passarowitz (1718). A hundred years previously, the Ottomans had been forced to come to terms with the Austrians at the treaty of Sitva Torok (1606). This had been a fairly advantageous treaty for the Ottomans, but in one respect it was a humiliation in that they were required to accept the Habsburg ruler as 'Roman Emperor' rather than the previous Ottoman usage of casually referring to him as 'the King of Vienna'. This was a recognition of a Christian state on the basis of equality, a true treaty rather than a truce dictated by the sultan to a frontier princeling. The treaties of Carlowitz and Passarowitz were far more humiliating in that the Ottomans lost territory which had been Ottoman for generations.

In the wake of these treaties there came the so-called Tulip Period (1703–30) in which western ideas were allowed into the Empire. The veil which had insulated the Ottomans from infidel ways was lifted just a little and, for the first time, positive steps were taken to open up the Ottoman territories to non-Ottoman ideas. The sultan sent a bureaucrat who had risen through the Janissary corps, Yirmisekiz Mehmed Chelebi Efendi, as ambassador to France with a mandate 'to study and report on those means of civilization and education which could be applicable here'.[4] The embassy had little direct impact on the Ottomans but it was symbolic of the change in thinking which had occurred in the ruling élite. A number of westerners were to come into the Empire and they introduced projects for institutions, particularly military ones, based on western models. In the end these came to nothing. However, what did come about from the embassy was a curious cultural exchange between France and the Ottoman Empire. With the failure of the second siege of Vienna in 1683, the Ottoman Empire was no longer seen as a threat to the whole of Western Europe and became the object of curiosity. With Yirmisekiz Mehmed Chelebi Efendi's embassy there came to France a large retinue of outlandishly dressed foreigners in turbans, caftans and pelisses which started a wave of *Turquerie* in France. Conversely, distinctly European styles were influencing the native architecture of the Ottomans, clearly seen in the rococo features in the fountain built by Ahmed III outside Topkapi Palace in this period (plate 32) and in the Nurosmaniye Mosque built by his successor, Mahmud I. At the same time one of the first of the Orientalists, Jean Baptiste Vanmour (1671–1737), came to Istanbul in 1703 together with the French ambassador De Ferriol. He painted a vast number of European visitors, mainly connected with the various embassies, and, if he did not initiate, he at least developed the fashion for Europeans having themselves portrayed in oriental costume. His book of engravings of Ottoman costumes, first published in 1712–13, was soon to go into two further printings to meet popular demand in Europe.[5] What was astonishing for the period was that the members of the Ottoman court, including the sultan himself, allowed themselves to be painted by this infidel. The explanation could be that he was seen as a craftsman and his handiwork was no threat to the Ottoman-system, indeed many of the craftsmen in the Empire were Christian. However, when it came to military and other sciences it was generally western converts to Islam who introduced new ideas, for the defence of the Sublime State was the responsibility of Muslims and not the Christian minorities, let alone western infidels.

In 1730 there was a revolt in Istanbul, partly in response to a major defeat on the Persian front and partly as a reaction to the lavish conspicuous consumption of the court and the introduction of infidel innovations. It seems that the court was prepared to accept foreign ideas but the people by and large wanted nothing to do with the West. The Empire once again drew the veil of seclusion around itself and enjoyed decades of comparative peace while Europe was preoccupied with the War of the Austrian Succession and the Seven Years War. Unaware of European affairs, most Ottomans saw this respite as further proof of the certainty that the Ottoman way was the best.

The Empire was awakened from this idyll by the Russian War of 1768 and the Treaty of Kuchuk Kaynarja which ended it in 1774. During the war the Russian fleet entered the Mediterranean, destroyed the Ottoman fleet, raised a rebellion in the Greek provinces and encouraged Egypt to act independently of Istanbul. The shock of having the Russians on their western flank rather than in the east and north was enough to persuade many Ottomans of rank of the need for reform. Even the more complacent could not help but become alarmed by the terms of the Treaty of Kuchuk Kaynarja. This document was to become a watershed in Ottoman history. Among the many provisions in the treaty two items were to have a profound implication for the future of the Ottoman Empire: Russia was conceded a particular position as protector of the Orthodox nation, and the Crimea, an area inhabited by Muslim Tatars, was to become autonomous. Not only had the Ottomans lost a predominantly Muslim area but the Russians had now acquired the right to interfere in the relations between the Ottoman government and its Orthodox subjects, a relationship based on the Holy Law and beyond the dictates of outsiders, particularly infidels. The Ottomans had emerged from the Middle Ages and, if somewhat belatedly and reluctantly, joined the modern world.

Reform had now become a necessity if the Ottoman State was to survive. Abdulhamid I (1774–89) began to invite foreigners into the Empire to train specialised corps in the army, such as the artillery and the engineers. This time there was no demand made that they should convert to Islam. The Ottomans were prepared to take advice from infidels. However, that was only in matters of a military nature where it was indisputable that the Ottoman military tactics were no match for the European ones. In other matters the Ottoman analysis of the reasons for decline were much more simplistic. The Ottoman State had abandoned the principles laid down by Suleyman and if only the order that had prevailed at that time could be re-established then the Empire would once again be strong. The traditional dichotomy between Men of the Sword, the Christian-born ruling élite, and the Men of the Pen, the Muslim-born scholarly élite, had ceased to be a reality for over a century. One of the problems identified by the Grand Vizier, Halil Hamid, was the fact that members of society were not wearing the clothes appropriate to their rank as prescribed by Suleyman's codification. Since the Tulip Period, earlier in the century, Ottomans had taken to wearing garments influenced by European and Persian styles. Orders were issued that these innovative fashions were to be abandoned. This was a naïve attempt somehow to reinstate the classical categories within Ottoman society by making people wear the classical garments. These first attempts at reform floundered in the mire of court politics where the sultan was not strong enough to impose his will upon the various factions vying for power. It needed a much stronger sultan to do this, and he emerged in 1789 in the person of Selim III.

Selim III (1779–1807) began his reign by inviting over twenty prominent men of the Empire to write memoranda on the reasons for weakness of the Empire and proposals for its reform. From all the suggestions that were made the consensus was that the army, built around the nucleus of the Janissary corps, had to be reformed. The main disagreement was how this was to be achieved. Typically, there were those who believed that a return to the methods and order of Suleyman's reign would accomplish the task. The more realistic argued that unless the traditional corps were retrained and re-equipped they would never be a match for European armies. A third view put forward the idea that a completely new army had to be established along European lines and the old army left to atrophy and finally be abolished. The sultan adopted the third option, and a new army was recruited. What was significant was that the new army was dressed in a uniform based on western models. The next fifteen years saw the modernisation of various corps in the army and the training of officers in western science. In this period many young Ottomans were sent abroad in the retinue of ambassadors, and they not only learnt foreign languages but began reading foreign literature and acquiring ideas alien to the Ottoman mind. Above all, French influence dominated in Istanbul and even Napoleon's invasion of Egypt in 1799 only put a temporary stop to relations with France. It is from this period that Ottoman society began to diverge into two distinct ideological paths. The young reformers, albeit dressed in oriental garments, had acquired access to foreign languages and ideas and were impatient for greater and more wide-ranging reforms, while the vast mass of Ottoman society was opposed to, when not totally unaware of, the changes that were taking place. However slow the pace of reform might have been for the modernisers it was far too rapid for most people, especially for those elements of society with a vested interest in keeping things the way they were. In 1807, Selim attempted to convert a corps of traditional auxiliary troops into a western-type regiment and issued them with European-styled uniforms. They mutinied and, joining up with the Janissaries, marched on Istanbul, toppled the sultan and put an end not only to the reform movement but eventually to Selim himself who was murdered in the palace. In his place, his cousin, Mustafa IV, was placed on the throne. The forces of reaction had won but only briefly for in the following year the reformers, who were vastly outnumbered, cleverly schemed to have Mustafa deposed and killed and his brother Mahmud enthroned in his place.

Mahmud II (1808–39) was a committed proponent of reform and wasted no time in attempting to re-establish all the institutions of reform that had been swept away by the reactionaries. Unfortunately he overestimated his own power and underestimated the fury of the Janissaries who mutinied once again and toppled the reformers in the government. Mahmud was saved from assassination by virtue of his being the only surviving male of the House of Osman. Mahmud had learnt a painful lesson, but it was a lesson that he was to learn well: if he were to reform the Empire he would have to reform more than just the military; other aspects of society would have to change. He also now realised that he must be thoroughly prepared before foisting innovation on a conservative society and to do so he must first destroy the opposition to reform. The next eighteen years were spent in preparation for the new reforms. Throughout this period the westerner would have seen little to suggest that the agenda for reforms had not been entirely abandoned. The Empire was as it had always been, the mysterious East resembling more the Arabian Nights than a European power.

Meanwhile the governor of Egypt, Muhammad Ali Pasha, began to reform Egypt in a way that was to become a model for later reforms in Istanbul. It is ironic that although Istanbul was closer to the West geographically, Egypt was to overtake the capital in terms of westernisation. Once he had destroyed the Mamelukes, the Egyptian establishment (1811–12), he had a free hand to create his own army from the *fellahin* and import foreign personnel to train them in the European arms with which they were equipped. The obvious success of Muhammad Ali's reforms was a further incentive to Mahmud to confront the Janissaries.

In the eighteen years that Mahmud held back from the confrontation he consolidated Ottoman power in the provinces of Anatolia and Rumelia, which for decades had resisted any interference from Istanbul. While Selim's logic had been that he should have complete control of Istanbul (i.e. the various factions including the Janissaries) before he could hope to subjugate the provinces, Mahmud first set about regaining power in the provinces and, building on that strength, then establishing himself as master in his own capital. Mahmud's preparations were being made to the background of the disastrous Greek War of Independence in which his army was so incapable of handling the situation that he was forced to call in his vassal Muhammad Ali

Pasha of Egypt whose modernised army performed very much better than the shambles that passed for the Janissary corps. By 1826 Mahmud was ready. The Janissaries, now discredited by their performance in the Greek War, had also become extremely unpopular in Istanbul. Mahmud had unobtrusively trained a modern army and when he was assured of support from the various factions in Istanbul he set out to provoke a mutiny by decreeing that a new force was to be set up from within the Janissary corps and that they were to be issued with new weapons and uniforms. This was enough to entice the Janissaries to open revolt, but this time Mahmud was prepared and ready. He surrounded the Janissaries in their barracks and massacred them, an event which was immediately termed the 'auspicious incident'.

Now that the opposition to reform had been eliminated, Mahmud was free to completely reform the whole administration of the Empire. He immediately introduced a new army with European uniforms, except for head-dress, for it was unthinkable to adopt the head-dress of the infidel. The fez was introduced after a suitable discussion as to whether it was truly an Islamic form of head-dress (it was). In 1829, it was decreed that all officials would henceforth dress in the new Ottoman dress: a fez to replace the turban, a frock coat to replace the caftan, tight trousers in place of the baggy shalwars, boots instead of slippers and a cape instead of the old pelisse. Overnight the government of the Ottoman Empire had ceased to look like the illustrations from the *Arabian Nights* and had the appearance of modern, if somewhat unfamiliar, Europeans. Exempted from the dress reforms were the religious dignitaries, teachers and judges; the scholarly institution. With a change in dress there came a change in manners and furniture. Tables and chairs were introduced and the sultan himself adopted international diplomatic conventions and began to stand up and greet ambassadors rather than have them forcibly prostrated flat on the ground in his presence as he sat cross-legged on the throne. These changes gained Mahmud the sobriquet 'the infidel sultan'.

At this period several events coincided to change the way that the West was to view the Ottoman Empire. The first of these was the Ottoman-Egyptian war of 1831–3. Muhammad Ali (plate 10) had requested the sultan that he be given the governorship of Syria and when this was refused he not only invaded Syria but marched on Istanbul. Mahmud sent an army against the Egyptian force but this was defeated and the road to Istanbul was no longer defended. Mahmud was at a loss as to how to stop his vassal from taking over the Empire by capturing Istanbul. The Russians intervened with an offer of an army which would protect Istanbul from the Egyptians. A treaty was signed at Hunkyar Iskelesi (1833) which was seen in Western Europe as the vehicle by which the Russians would emerge as the dominant force in the Ottoman Empire. From this point onwards, Palmerston adopted a policy of supporting the Ottoman Empire to prevent any possibility of Russia becoming stronger at the expense of the Ottomans. Henceforth the Eastern Question (i.e. what to do with the Ottoman Empire) came on the agenda of British foreign policy. Greater and greater reforms were demanded from what became a reluctant Ottoman government which was not always clear as to where the reforms would lead. Meanwhile in Europe sentiment towards the Turks had changed considerably. In the Age of Reason the prevailing mythology (for mythology it was) saw them as a barbaric force enslaving Christian populations, especially the Greeks who were the heirs to an ancient and noble culture. By the third decade of the nineteenth century, at the height of the Romantic period, they were seen as harmless objects of curiosity, a medieval society on the brink of modernisation worthy of visual record before it disappeared completely in the modern world. The age of Orientalism had arrived. The demands of the reform movement meant that foreigners had increasingly greater access to the Ottoman Empire and it was placed firmly on the itinerary of the Grand Tour.

When Abdulmejid (fig 19) came to the throne in 1839, the Ottoman Empire was once again facing a crisis. Muhammad Ali was again threatening to attack Istanbul.[6] This time the various powers, uneasy at France's support of the Egyptian governor and its increasing influence there, joined together to force Muhammad Ali to back down. The French, increasingly isolated diplomatically, withdrew their support and Muhammad Ali not only withdrew from Syria but conceded to other demands made by the sultan. This was at a price, and what was demanded of the Ottoman government was further reform. To secure the support of the western powers the new sultan was forced to issue the Imperial Rescript of Gulhane (1839), in which, among other measures, he allowed equality before the law to all subjects, including non-Muslims, a legislative council and financial reform. Equality of Muslim and non-Muslim was impossible, a legislative council was nothing short of blasphemous because there was only the God-given Holy Law and it was the task of lawyers to interpret it, not to add or subtract from it. The *Kanuns* issued by the sultan from time to time had had the effect of legislation but were, theoretically, merely codifications of earlier practices. As for the financial reforms, they were to stabilise the currency in the short term[7] but ended up bankrupting the Empire as loan after loan was sought to cover previous borrowings. The aim of these reforms was not to make the Ottoman State better able to defend itself but to make trading conditions more favourable for foreigners. Whatever the effects of these reforms Ottoman industry collapsed during this period. Ubicini, in his *Letters on Turkey*, published in 1856, noted:

Manufacturing industry has greatly declined from what it formerly was in the Ottoman Empire. At present the greater part of the exports of Turkey consist in raw materials, which it hands over to Europe, and which the latter returns to Turkey in a manufactured form. The numerous and varied manufactures, which formerly sufficed not only for the consumption of the empire, but also stocked the markets of all the Levant, and of several countries in Europe, no longer exist or have completely declined.[8]

These reforms and trading opportunities brought more foreigners to Istanbul and the district of Pera (present-day Beyoglu) which expanded rapidly to accommodate them. The collapse of the revolutions of 1848 brought many refugees from Central Europe to Istanbul and the Crimean War in the next decade made the Ottoman Empire the object of curiosity in the West and created a steady market for images of the East.

As for the Ottoman, they lurched from one crisis to the next through the remainder of the century, society totally split between the progressives who wanted westernisation at any cost and the conservatives who questioned the benefits of these reforms. They questioned the benefits of materialism, the inevitability of nationalism and whether, after all, the Ottoman way had not been better.

1 Niccolò Machiavelli, *The Prince*, trans. George Bull, Harmondsworth, 1961, p.45.

2 *The Turkish Letters of Ogier de Busbecq, Imperial Ambassador at Constantinople, 1554–1562*, trans. E. S. Forster, Oxford, 1968, p.61.

3 Ibid., pp.60–1.

4 Quoted by Ziya Karal in 'Tanzimattan Evvel Garplilasma hareketleri' in *Tanzimat*, Istanbul, 1940, p.19.

5 Ibid.

6 This crisis prevented David Wilkie from travelling directly to the Holy Land and forced him to remain in Istanbul where he did several portraits and studies.

7 It was as part of the currency reforms that James Robertson was brought over to Istanbul to work in the Imperial Mint as an engraver.

8 M. A. Ubicini, *Letters on Turkey*, trans. Lady Easthope, London, 1856, II, p.339.

The Painter's Vision

Julie Lawson

AFTER the conception and before the realisation of Antoine Watteau's painting, *Fêtes Vénitiennes* (plate 1), there was a change of plan. It is possible to discern beneath the present paint surface the ghost of his first idea. Originally, the couple were yet to take the first step upon their dance. At some point, Watteau decided that the courtship between the gentleman in eastern costume and the lady in western should have begun. The love affair between East and West – between strangers – should set out on its unpredictable course.

For centuries, the East has been more than simply a matter of geography for the western imagination. It has represented a set of possibilities that are not conceivable at home. Thoughts and feelings about the East have been elaborated, since the coming of Islam, with the same kind of obsessional poetic purpose that saw the artistic attempt at retrieval of the Arcadia of the West.

The eighteenth and nineteenth centuries were the period which saw the most complete realisation of the fantasy of the East. The tenor of fantasy that is the signature of Orientalism was set by the art of the rococo, and was cheerfully continued in the empirical Age of Reason. But Orientalism is most importantly an aspect of Romanticism. As will be seen, the rich and sometimes lurid image of the East paled by the light of utilitarian enquiry as the nineteenth century wore on.

The spirit of the East sometimes invaded the world of the eighteenth-century French painter Antoine Watteau. He was the inventor of the *fête galante*: a scene of youthful dalliance, set out of doors, where the garden of a château meets the park beyond. The young people who flirt and fall in love there are suspended between the constraints of civilisation and the freedom of nature. The voice of Reason is still just audible, but so are the pipes of Pan. This is the case for the protagonists of the *Fêtes Vénitiennes.* They dress as characters of the commedia dell'arte and are to be thought of as acting their parts. Watteau mixes love-making, dressing-up and play-acting, in order to create for us an essentially ambiguous set of circumstances. The crucial question of lovers' sincerity has no certain answer. However, there is a person here who is alien to even these uncertain norms. The man in oriental costume stands on the periphery of the small dramas of love enacted by the characters of the commedia. This Turk has been bold in his choice at the costumiers. He has chosen the unfamiliar, the passionate part, and his courtship is serious, perhaps even sinister, compared with the casual importuning of some of the others. As well as by his costume, he is isolated from the rest of the action by the funnel of trees above and the sky behind him. If the party takes place at the limits of the garden, he is to be thought of as having come from the park, from the wilder place. The essential characteristics of Orientalist art are prefigured in this painting: in ambiguity, in the assumption of disguise, in standing beyond the confines of convention, and in the paradox of passion and alienation.

The nineteenth-century French novelists and art critics Edmond and Jules de Goncourt wrote of paintings by Watteau:

... when you have traversed the rivers, the hills, the garden walks, when you have passed the lakes and the fountains, then the Paradise of Watteau opens before you. It is Cythera. Beneath a sky painted with the colours of summer, the galley of Cleopatra sways at the water's grassy edge.[1]

Artists looking to the East are always, in a sense, responding to Watteau's dream, trying to rediscover this lost Eden, this 'Luxe, calme et volupté'.

The European artists who looked to the regions of the Ottoman Empire for their subject-matter were also, to a greater or lesser extent, pursuing their own concerns, even when ostensibly examining those of another culture. They used eastern themes to explore western preoccupations. When they have attempted to be most objective, they have revealed themselves most unwittingly. Paradox, ambivalence and ambiguity mark the western interest in the East and make complicated a discussion of the art which takes it as its subject.

The western view of the East in the eighteenth century was balanced between hostility and admiration. Ottoman Turkey – a traditional enemy – was known and admired for the sophistication of its arts and crafts. It was associated with calligraphy, bookbinding, gorgeous fabrics, carpets and ceramics. Emblematic of the peaceful arts had been the cultivation of the tulip, imported to Europe in the seventeenth century. Originated in Persia and grown in Turkey for pleasure, when it arrived in the West it acquired a confused and ambiguous status as both a thing of delight and an object reduced to the utilitarianism of the market, where it was traded by eager speculators. And where more appropriate for western intellectuals to discuss the ironies of such phenomena than in the coffee house, foregathered in direct emulation of their philosophical eastern counterparts?

And yet, the stereotype of the 'cruel Turk' coexisted with that of the sophisticate. It survived well into the nineteenth century, long after the Empire in its decline and decadence had ceased to offer any real threat to the West. The persistence and the nature of this myth is of particular interest. It is based largely, as Edward Said has shown, on notions fraught with assumptions of superiority – of culture, race and religion – on the part of western writers.[2] For this their works have been castigated as symptomatic of an unattractive and offensive cultural imperialism.

At the very heart of the myth of the East lies paradox and ambivalence – fascination and fear, attraction and repulsion. Myths, however, are not primarily instrumental; they do not shape or direct experience in a specific and mechanistic way. They do not mould it with the filigree patterns of absolute particularity. Myths are, rather, catalytic or enabling – perhaps even necessary in order for experience to be possible.

The consideration of the East in terms of representation and misrepresentation is a crucial task for others much better equipped to undertake it. The purpose here is, rather, to block in the colours and sketch the outlines of a recurring idea in western art that catches shiftingly, and often diffidently, the reflection of the East, and serves to contrast with a grey, rationalistic and utilitarian West.

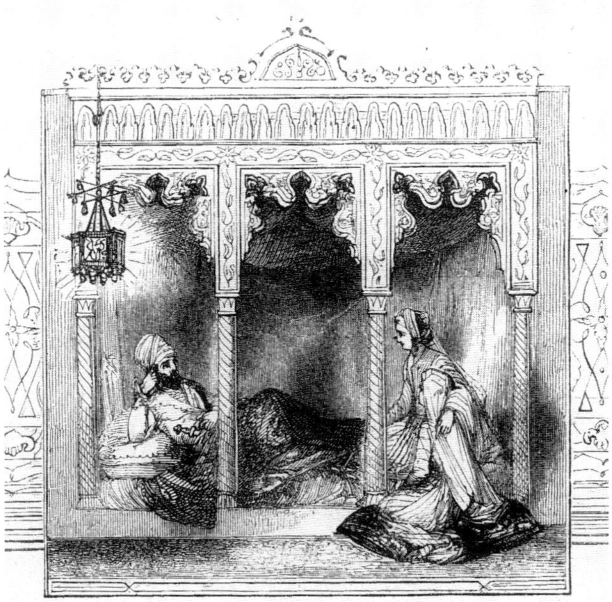

FIG 1
Sheherazade Narrating her Stories, illustration by Owen Jones from Edward William Lane's *The Thousand and One Nights; or, The Arabian Nights' Entertainments* 1847
(National Library of Scotland, Edinburgh)

THE BYRONIC ORIENT: THE GOAL OF IMAGINATION

Most western Europeans in the eighteenth and nineteenth centuries were introduced to the 'Orient' through the *Arabian Nights.*[3] This was the most prevalent source of popular ideas about the Islamic world. The stories are an amalgam of the fantastic and the plausible, gaining a strong sense of reality through the vivid description of tangible objects. As a recent Orientalist scholar, Leila Ahmed expresses it:

The tales were set in a world as remote and unreal as that of dream, and so they were insulated from the world of ordinary daily experience by their setting as well as by their nature ... It was the vagueness of that world, of the physical objects and manners referred to: veils, harems, sultans, genii ... and their existence in detachment from their specific significance to their own culture, that made it possible for the English writers imitating the Arabian Nights tales to borrow them to clothe their own vision.[4]

She notes the paradox of 'the richness of vivid concrete detail that forms part of the texture of the Nights', which were, however, 'experienced above all on an imaginative plane'. As a world that was, therefore, perceived as both real and unreal at the same time, 'the Oriental world became established as the metaphor for the realities of dream, of imagination and, eventually, of poetry'.

Western travellers would constantly declare that their first encounter with the Near East was like stepping into scenes from the *Arabian Nights.* They 'recognised' the people and places because they had read about and imagined them. So, superficially at least, the fantasy and the reality were indistinguishable.

The paradoxical myth of the passionate and luxurious Turk was perpetuated by the art of the nineteenth century. For Lord Byron, the most influential poet of the first two decades of the century, the myth contained more possibilities and scope for the poetic imagination than mundane reality. 'Byronic Orientalism' exerted such a powerful influence upon the popular imagination, and upon a generation of writers and artists, that its nature and allure should be explored.

Know ye the land where the cypress and myrtle
Are emblems of deeds that are done in their clime?
Where the rage of the vulture, the love of the turtle,
Now melt into sorrow, now madden to crime!

Byron, *The Bride of Abydos, Canto I, 1–8*

The *Turkish Tales* were written after Byron's return from the East in 1811.[5] They were poems of violence, of vengeful and hot-blooded Turks, excesses of passion and cold-hearted cruelty. He wrote in his Journal on 5 December 1813, that his poem, *The Bride of Abydos* (published a few days earlier): '... wrung my thoughts from reality to imagination – from selfish regrets to vivid recollections – and recalled me to a country replete with the *brightest* and *darkest*, but always most *lively* colours of my memory'.[6] For Byron, emotions relived in a state of nervous excitement served to produce the poetry that was to epitomise the darker side of Romanticism.

What Byron called the 'horrible imaginings' of the *Turkish Tales,*[7] and the nature of their subject matter, were a cause of concern to many. A typical criticism was that Byron '... delights too exclusively in the delineation of a certain morbid exaltation of character and feeling, – a sort of demoniacal sublimity, not without some traits of the ruined Archangel'.[8] Byron never denied the darker side of Nature. The morbid and sublime were, for him, inside Nature, not in a separate realm of darkness.

Byron had travelled and acquired first-hand knowledge of the Near East. But, as a poet, he chose the licence of imagination rather than acquiescence in the authority of fact. As was proper to the art according to Johnson, he did not 'number the streaks of the tulip'.[9] In reality, however, Byron's experience of the Turks was not so very lurid:

If it be difficult to pronounce what they [the Ottomans] *are, we can at least say what they are not; they are not treacherous, they are not cowardly, they do not burn heretics, they are not assassins, nor has an enemy advanced to their capital. They are faithful to their sultan till he becomes unfit to govern, and devout to their God without an inquisition. Were they driven from St Sophia tomorrow, and the French or Russians enthroned in their stead, it would become a question whether Europe would gain by the exchange. England would certainly be the loser.*[10]

Here speaks a member of the British Upper House of Parliament.

Byron the politician was not the same as Byron the poet. It was over the question of Greece that Byron, in ideological terms, criticised Turkey. All of the preceding remarks about the Turks were by way of explanation to one line of his poem *Childe Harold's Pilgrimage* in which Greece is described as 'Trembling beneath the scourge of Turkish hand'. Byron was at pains to explain that his dislike was not of the Turks *per se*; rather he was opposed to a tyranny exercised by the Turkish government and his stance was an anti-imperialist one. He saw a

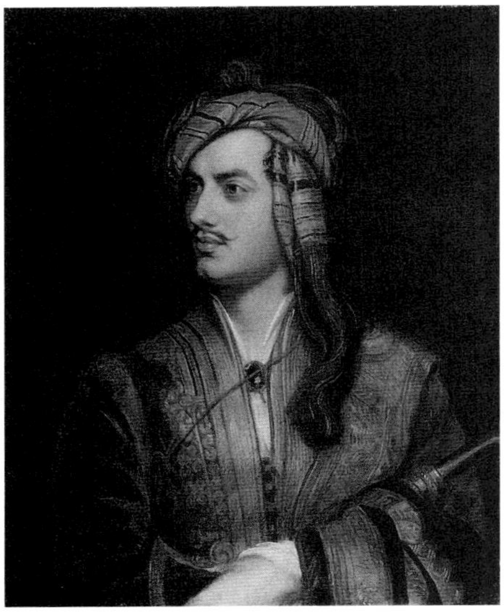

FIG 2 THOMAS PHILLIPS
Lord Byron 1835 (after a portrait of 1813)
(National Portrait Gallery, London)

parallel with the relationship between England and Ireland.[11] It was on philosophical grounds that he championed the Greeks against oppression, impelled by a belief in the right of nationhood and perhaps a Romantic dislike of *force majeure.* Byron's notions of political independence and nationalism were essentially Romantic. He opposed tyranny however it manifested itself, and, as the splenetic cynicism of his comparison of Greece and Ireland displays, he was often using the injustices embodied in one set of circumstances abroad to criticise those closer to home. For Byron, there was no incompatibility between his role as poet and his stance as philosopher or politician. Certainly, the rationalism of the philosopher or the pragmatism of the politician were not to lead the poet by the nose, and he would have agreed with Shelley that poets are 'the true legislators of the world'.

Byron's Orient was essentially a fictional one – a place of myth and fantasy. Escapism is a significant element of Orientalism, and 'dressing up', adopting a disguise, is a kind of escaping. In Byron's case, he adopted a costume in the East that had heroic associations with a ferocious and bellicose tribe, the Arnaouts, or Albanians, renowned for bravery in battle (fig2). He likened the Arnaouts to the Highlanders of Scotland and indeed, his own sense of Scottishness – even to the extent of wearing tartan – came to the fore when he was in the East.[12]

Byron's dressing up was part of the creation of a persona, a fictional self. He was the archetypical Romantic in this sense – setting himself outside cultural and conventional boundaries. The Arnaout costume in which he posed for the portrait by Thomas Phillips does indeed state an allegiance, and, as such, has a 'real' significance; but it is also part of a kind of fiction. Artists can adopt different voices: the words and philosophies of their protagonists are not necessarily their own. Contemporary critics observed that Byron's heroes all seemed to merge into one. Of course, this was generally taken to be the poet himself – not in the strictly autobiographical sense – but a fictive self, a projection. The portrait of Byron by Phillips represents Byron the Orientalist.

Sir Walter Scott was able to disentangle the poet from the politician. Whilst he disapproved of the latter, and disliked the 'misanthropical ennui'[13] that, for him, made Byron's work morally reprehensible, he recognised Byron's genius and defended his poetry against some of the more uncomprehending critics. In response to the criticism levelled at Byron that his poetry suffered from a certain roughness of expression resulting from the rapidity of his production -what in painting would be seen as a lack of 'finish' – Scott explained: '... such is the deep and powerful strain of passion, such the original tone and colouring of description, that the want of polish in some of its minute parts rather adds to than deprives the poem of its energy'.[14]

To an extent, Byron's Orientalism is based on observation; but it is not to do with merely recounting experiences. With regard to 'Oriental' poetry Scott opined:

... it is not enough for the representation of an eastern landscape, that the foreground should be encumbered with turbans and sabres, and the fantastic architecture of the kiosk or the mosque, if the distance be not marked by those slight but discriminating touches which mark the reality of the scene, the lightly indicated palm-tree, which overhangs the distant fountain, or the shadowy and obscure delineation of the long column of the caravan retreating through the distance ...[15]

Byron's indifference to the facts of the matter is a poetic necessity. To render concrete and tangible through excessive detail is to render prosaic and poetry must convey authenticity of feeling as well as atmosphere and a sense of place. The picture can be sketched in, to be completed in the imagination of the beholder. Byron had suggested as much when he wrote to Thomas Moore, author of the 'Eastern' poem *Lalla Rookh*: 'You have caught the colours as if you had been in the rainbow, and the tone of the East is perfectly preserved' adding that '... it requires something more than to have been upon the hunch of a dromedary to compose a good Oriental story ...'.[16] Unlike many authors, Scott noted, Byron did not forget '... that it is his business rather to excite than to satiate the imagination of his readers'.[17]

The French artist Eugène Delacroix was inspired by the poetry of Byron to paint some of his greatest works. (plates 2–4) Like Byron, he was a controversial genius. He was applauded and reviled, and recognised in his lifetime by some – in particular by the poet and art critic, Baudelaire – as the greatest French Romantic painter. Like Byron's, his rapid and vehement working methods were an essential part of his creative process, and determined the essential characteristics of his style.

Delacroix's temperament is particularly revealed in his graphic work. Drawing brings us as close as it is possible to come to the private artist and the workings of his mind. We confront the immediacy of his original ideas and feelings as he gave them expression. Particularly, in certain preparatory drawings, the artist's hand and mind are working in synchrony. Some of Delacroix's most expressive achievements are the drawings related to his paintings of *The Giaour*, a Byronic subject that Delacroix returned to and reworked throughout his career (plate 3 and fig 3).

The inspiration was Byron's poem of the same name, described by the poet as 'the adventure of a female slave, who was thrown, in the Mussulman manner, into the sea for infidelity, and avenged by a young Venetian, her lover'.[18] However, Delacroix does not illustrate Byron. Rather, he uses the poetry as a release for his own creative imaginings. The action, exotic setting, and the visual imagery in the poetry, combined with the power and rawness of the passions expressed, all become an inspiration for Delacroix, a kind of emotional springboard. He has sought visual equivalents in his paintings for the powerful imagery, the changing rhythms and cascading torrents of words in the poem. The energy and vivid detail is emulated in the flowing and dynamic handling, and in the colour.

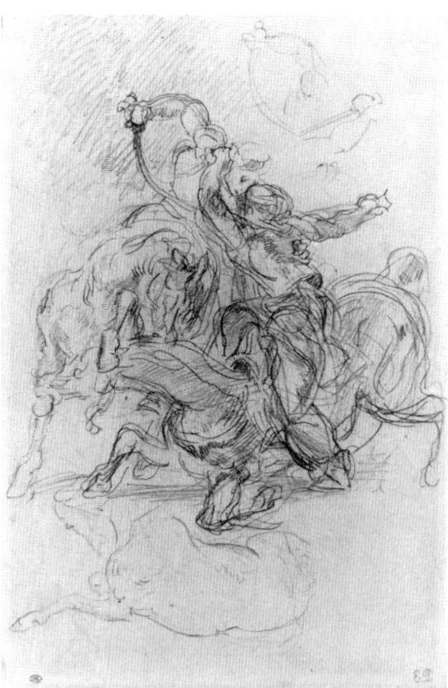

FIG 3 EUGENE DELACROIX
Two Oriental Horsemen in Combat c.1835
(Musée du Louvre, Paris)

Another of Byron's works provided an even more celebrated inspiration. An account survives of Delacroix's first response to the dénouement of Byron's verse drama, *The Death of Sardanapalus*: *C'était une scène qui s'était d'abord présentée à son imagination, empreinte de deuil et d'horreur. Il avait pris la palette sous cette impression; en quelques heures, une esquisse d'une caractère énergique et sombre avait apparu sous son pinceau …*[19]
[It was a scene which came at once to his imagination, an impression of death and horror. Affected in this way, he took up his palette; within a few hours a sketch of a spirited and sombre character had appeared beneath his paintbrush] (plate 2).

Whatever the accuracy of this account, the essential point must be true. It is that Delacroix's response to the poetry was so strong that it induced in him a heightened state of mind, out of which was created the work of art. This is akin to the ancient idea of a divine frenzy, and it is not difficult to associate Delacroix with the Dionysiac principle. The work could even be said to be untrue to Byron's conception, so much is it a product of an inflamed imagination. Delacroix worked on the finished painting for a year, elaborating and enlarging it but the essential idea was there at its creation.[20]

The story is of Sardanapalus, the king of Nineveh and Assyria, a follower of the god Bacchus, who calls for wine as the enemy besieges his capital. He declares a revel to be 'better than a trophy, / Being bought without a tear' (I, 196–7). Sardanapalus is a paradox. He is a lover of beauty, civilised and refined in his tastes – a sensualist. Byron describes him as 'effeminately dressed, his head crowned with flowers, and his robe negligently flowing'. This epicurean who has neglected the arts of war for those of peace is, however, in the painting, capable of the savagery and remorselessness of destroying the things he loved. He makes a funeral pyre that will consume him and his palace, declaring that 'In this blazing palace / And its enormous walls of reeking ruin, / We leave a nobler monument than Egypt / Hath piled in her brick mountains, o'er / dead kings …' (I, 480 ff)

Delacroix's *The Death of Sardanapalus*, which was exhibited at the Salon of 1827–8, is a comprehensive inversion of familiar values. History

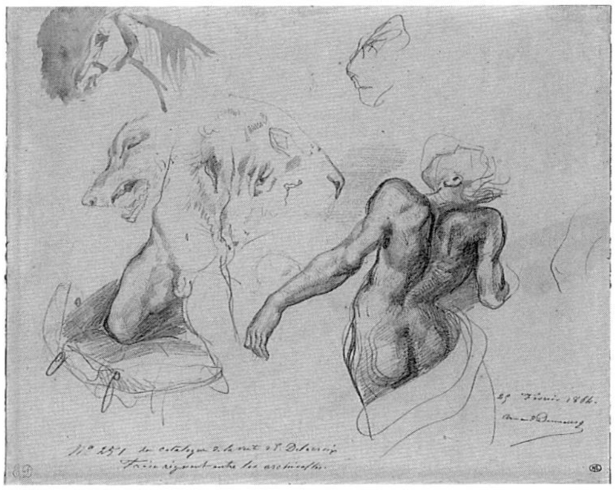

FIG 4 EUGENE DELACROIX
Sketch for The Death of Sardanapalus 1826–7
(Musée du Louvre, Paris)

painting, whose claim to pre-eminence among the genres rested on its ability to draw a strict and instructive connection between artistic values and those moral values upon which civilisation and the idea of nobility rested, is here subjected to a shocking and mystifying mutation. At the centre of the action is the anti-hero. Neither active, nor still and magisterial, he is a figure of languor. The centrifugal force that sees the destruction of his splendid possessions – jewels, steeds and concubines – is morally unaccountable in the terms with which the western epic is familiar.[21] Here, in this ancient East, the life of consumption must conclude, by an alien logic, with the destruction of everything that the appetite feasted upon. Delacroix has transgressed a boundary here. At this geographical and temporal remove, observing the action from some unstable height, moral bearings are lost. The restive oscillation between the call of the senses and the reins of the intellect, which is the curse of the Classical and Christian West, is here stilled. Inhibition is suspended, and an abandonment to terror and sensuality is invited. These are opposites in the ordinary world: terror repels and sensuality lures. At Sardanapalus's end – and beyond the West the painter implies – all is reversed.

There is a preparatory drawing for *The Death of Sardanapalus* that combines an agonised nude female figure, a powerful Michelangelesque male study and a wolf's head with a savage, snarling muzzle (fig 4). These shocking juxtapositions are revealing. They are honest because the sketch is an unselfconscious, private expression. The Romantic artist is audacious enough to confront the darker recesses of the soul. Delacroix explored the realm of the dark, 'Saracenic' Orientalism associated with Lord Byron.

LUXURY AND LIBERTY

The Orient for Romantic artists was a mechanism for the release of the imagination. It was a stimulation and a vehicle for their ideas and a source of new motifs. The 'orientals' they depicted were natural, elemental and passionate; untrammelled by the rules and regulations of a bourgeois civilisation; closer to the experience of the senses, and, by implication, anti-rational.

Delacroix and Byron treat the Orient as a place where the fetters of convention may be cast off and where the life of the senses is found to be the condition of human freedom. Western artists all, in varying ways, found the journey East, whether undertaken in imagination or in fact, a journey of liberation. This was already a familiar and potent concept by the nineteenth century. In the schematic map of the mind, the East was thought of as antithetical to the West.

The Orient was not, however, a unitary concept. As has been seen, cruelty and luxury were thought to be perversely compatible there. In addition, there were two essentially different concepts of the East which attracted artists of different temperaments and with differing concerns: these may be characterised emblematically as the 'East of the oasis' and the 'East of the desert'.

When he was in Istanbul in 1850, after his own journey to the Near East, the French writer Gustave Flaubert wrote:

Passing Abydos, I thought of Byron. That is his Orient, the Turkish Orient, the Orient of the curved sword, the Albanian costume, and the grilled window looking on the blue sea. I prefer the baked Orient of the bedouin and the desert … [22]

These two elemental 'edges' – water and sand – denote different aspects of Orientalism. They can be thought of literally and metaphorically. On the other side of these edges or boundaries, different sensations could be experienced and a different moral and rational terrain would be seen.

The 'baked' Orient was the goal of the painters who went east in search of the earth and fire, the elements of the Bible lands. Tracing the footsteps of the children of Israel out of Egypt, or John the Baptist in the wilderness, or Christ through his temptation, was an arduous expedition, for stoical individuals. Air and water, the matter of dreams of the Orient, made of the East a place of ease. If we go to the desert in search of memory, our desire at the oasis is to become amnesiacs. The poet's and the sybarite's goal was in the indolence or the moral relativism of the place of cool shades and fountains.

Lady Mary Wortley Montagu (fig 5) described

Turkey as the epitome of the oasis, a veritable earthly paradise. In 1717, she wrote to Alexander Pope, describing her summer retreat just outside Istanbul: *I am in the middle of a wood consisting chiefly of fruit trees, watered by a vast number of fountains, famous for the excellency of their water, and divided into many shady walks, upon short grass, that seems to me artificial, but, I am assured is the pure work of nature; and within view of the Black Sea, from whence we perpetually enjoy the refreshment of cool breezes that makes us insensible of the heat of summer.*[23]

The harem is the most potent symbol of the idea of the exoticism and 'otherness' associated with the East, conceived as the antithesis of the West. It is an idea which finds its most intellectually coherent and lucid expression in the odalisque paintings of Ingres. They are paintings in which Ingres aims to balance realism with the classical ideal – poised as they are between Classicism and Naturalism. Further, there is the ambition to create a perfect duality of the sensual, as both experience and as idea.

The theme is one that Ingres returned to and reworked throughout his career. One would hardly know that *The Valpinçon Bather* (1808, fig 6) is an odalisque – a woman of the harem. That she is, endows her with a physical and temporal reality in an 'Oriental' setting. She is not as carnal as Rubens's women, but she is as tangibly flesh and blood as Titian's great Venuses. However, it is significant that she is not the goddess Venus, a figure of supernatural beauty.

The *Odalisque with a Slave* (1842, fig 7) presents the idea of the complete and simultaneous gratification of all the senses. The woman luxuriates in her sensuality; she lies on silk, she smells the perfumes from the garden beyond, she hears music, she sees beautiful colours, trees, swans on the water. Her sensibilities have been heightened by opiates from the hookah she has lain aside, and she languishes in a torpor of satiety. The path she has taken to oblivion is not entirely different from that of Sardanapalus. In both cases, the defeat of sensuality is not by the

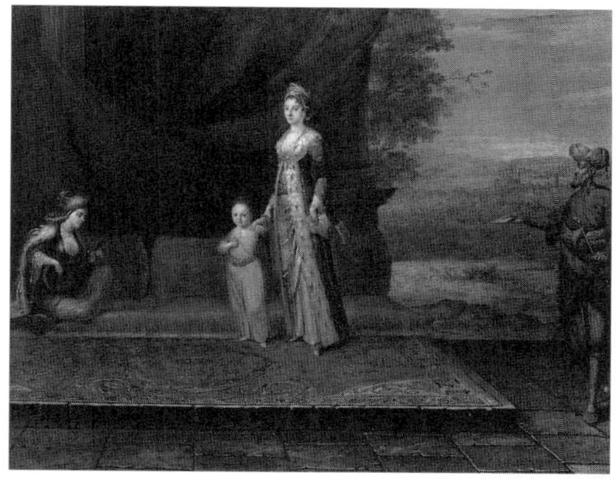

FIG 5 ATTRIBUTED TO JEAN-BAPTISTE VANMOUR
Lady Mary Wortley Montagu c.1716
(National Portrait Gallery, London)

FIGS 6, 7 & 8
JEAN AUGUSTE DOMINIQUE INGRES
The Valpinçon Bather 1808
(Musée du Louvre, Paris)
Odalisque with a Slave 1842
(Walters Art Gallery, Baltimore)
La Grande Odalisque 1814
(Musée du Louvre, Paris)

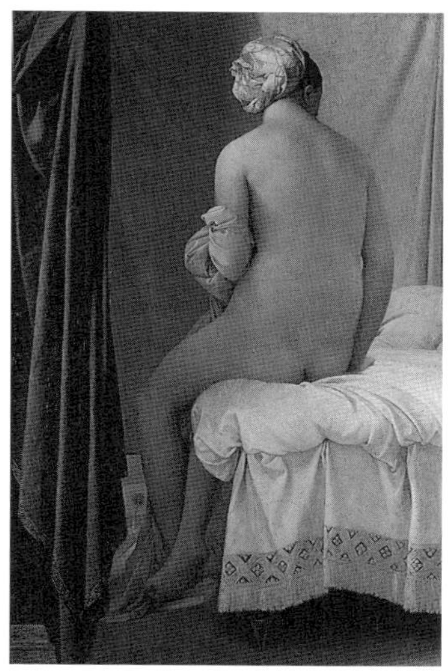

6

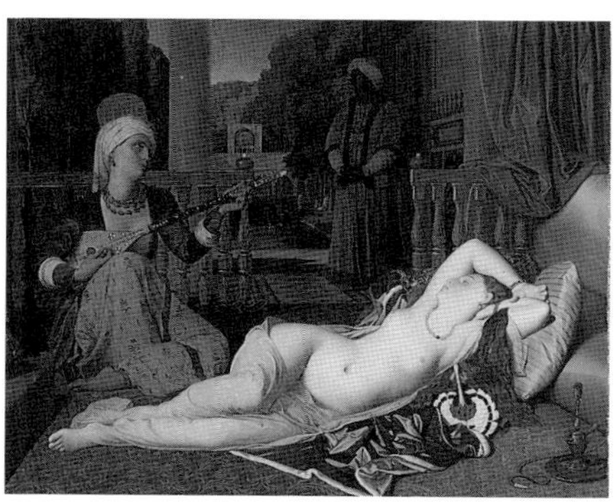

7

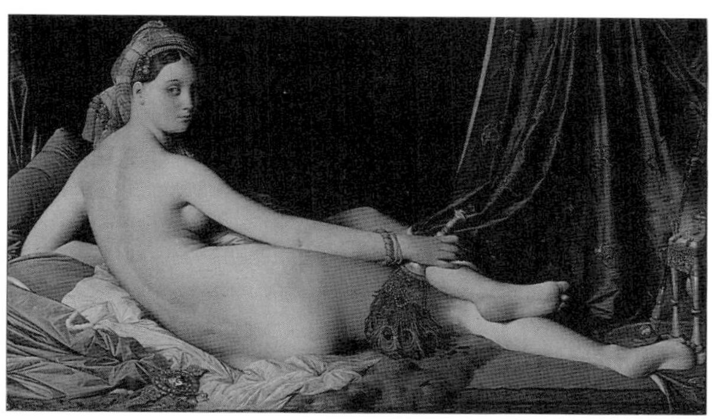

8

ascendency of reason, but by the annihilation of consciousness, through narcosis or death.

Mediating and balanced between the two is the *Grande Odalisque* (1814) (fig 8) in which the comprehensive sensuality of the *Odalisque with a Slave* is given a more abstract expression. The mass of gorgeous, hot colours is here a limited range of cool blues and greens, and the paraphernalia of the harem is reduced to one opium pipe and a peacock-feather fan. The woman is perfectly self-assured and poised in her sexuality. She looks at the viewer, conscious of being not only the subject of sensation, but the object of sensation too. Ingres is effectively proposing a condition in which there is no dualistic separation of the mind and the body. This condition – the painter suggests – would be a return to Eden, a rediscovery of the Golden Age, where such sensuality and innocent extroversion are not mutually exclusive. The Orient, and in particular, the harem, has been made to serve as a metaphor for this beatitude.

The female inhabitant of the harem has a counterpart. In opposition to the sequestered female is the unconstrained male. Delacroix is frequently the painter of the man whose life is lived exclusively in the action of the body. Sometimes he is engaged in the lion hunt, or in some other life-or-death struggle, all reason driven out of mind by the extreme physical violence of the moment.

The meeting of two opposing principles – action and passion, male and female, East and West – represents a perfect balance of the elements. It is a traditional western theme of art, a metaphor found in Renaissance art in the subject of Mars and Venus. When war is done and Mars comes together with his opposite,Venus, then the arts of peace can flourish. There will be love, music, poetry, peace and plenty. The odalisques of Ingres revive this metaphor, in non-mythological terms. Symbolically, the passionate, violent, male 'Turk' and the sensual, pacific, female odalisque would, together, represent a perfect condition. This is not so much the imposition of a western iconographical model on the East, as a use of the East as a metaphor for revitalising a constant western preoccupation.

Know ye the land of the cedar and vine,
Where the flowers ever blossom, the beams ever shine;
Where the light wings of Zephyr, oppress'd with perfume,
Wax faint o'er the gardens of Gul in her bloom;
Where the citron and olive are fairest of fruit,
And the voice of the nightingale never is mute:
Where the tints of the earth, and the hues of the sky,
In colour though varied, in beauty may vie,
And the purple of ocean is deepest in dye; ...

Byron, *The Bride of Abydos*, Canto I 9–13

THE ORIENT SEEN

There are different kinds of traveller – either imaginatively or actually. There are those who travel and carry with them a set of preconceptions and assumptions about other places and peoples, and who seek confirmation. There are others who travel to discover what was previously unknown, who travel innocently, unencumbered with a heavy baggage of ideas and attitudes. There is also a third traveller, perhaps an occasional companion of the first. This traveller is neither prejudiced nor naïve, but seeks in the East the basis of a critique of the West.

In the West, certain causal connections are seen generally to apply. They regulate, say, class relations, comprise a set of economic laws, dictate rules of conduct, underpin systems of value. They can seem necessary; that is, without alternative. A reason for travelling, in reality or imagination, is to find these connections *not* applying. The aim is to undermine arguments about the *necessary* nature of things. So, the search is on for alternative social and economic arrangements, for other histories, moralities or sets of aesthetic values. If they are found, they prove that western connections are conventional or pragmatic. And at last, a liberation of people from psychological and political norms may take place, and Romantic and Revolutionary purposes intersect.

Generally speaking, the Romantic liberation of the imagination attempted to evade the positivist discrimination of the factually true and false. The East was a place where the oppositions and contradictions of the West could seem to be cast in new terms, free of crisis. But this place was a poetic construct; it was designed for the convenience of the escapist, the fantasist and the political malcontent. Experience of the social and political reality, as has been seen, could be inconvenient, to the extent that Byron might have to write long, exonerating footnotes or Ingres might find it easier to stay at home.

The reality of the East, however, demanded to be integrated with the poetic fiction, especially if it was to serve as a practical corrective to some or other western state of error. The same applied to the state of ignorance: its alleviation required that the traveller attempt to observe with objectivity – an exercise of innocence, perhaps. In the eighteenth century, for example, Lady Mary Wortley Montagu had remarked – surprisingly – upon the relative freedom of women in Turkey:

I cannot forbear admiring, either the exemplary discretion or extreme stupidity of all the writers that have given accounts of them. ... Upon the whole, I look upon the Turkish women as the only free people in the Empire.[24]

Important changes took place as the nineteenth century progressed. Accounts of travels to the East proliferated, and the archaeological spirit that had existed since Europeans began to make the journey east at the end of the seventeenth century gathered momentum. The impetus given to Egyptology by the Napoleonic conquest was as effective in Britain as in France. A systematic, detailed examination of factual evidence was undertaken by the French, who conducted a codification and measurement of things Egyptian, from sphinxes to crocodiles. While the political motives should not be forgotten – and to codify is, in a sense, to possess – the scientific spirit in which the task was carried out was to set an example that many followed.[25] The subsequent publications by Baron Dominique-Vivant Denon demonstrate how closely allied archaeological aspirations and Romantic sensibilities were at the time (figs 9, 10).[26] In the visual arts, the archaeological spirit had its own tradition. In the eighteenth century, for example, James Dawkins and Robert Wood had taken the artist, Giovanni Battista Borra, to record their findings at Palmyra. Robert Adam had surveyed Diocletian's palace at Split, and Stuart and Revett had published *The Antiquities of Athens.* Gradually, as the nineteenth century progressed, this spirit became more prevalent. Denon's publications were widely read and must have been one of the greatest inspirations for subsequent travellers to Egypt.

The nineteenth century abounds with artists whose enthusiasm for the East was fired by an archaeological zeal. A typical example is the Scot, Robert Hay. In the 1820s and 1830s, he employed a group of architectural draughtsmen, including the Orientalist scholar Edward Lane, to accompany him and undertake an ambitious enterprise of recording, in minute detail, the monuments of Ancient Egypt. Testifying to the aim of accuracy in recording is their use of the camera lucida – an optical device that involved the use of a small prism and a lens through which the viewer could see an image on paper, thus facilitating the accurate drawing of the

FIG 9 BARON DOMINIQUE-VIVANT DENON
The Sphinx and the Pyramids 1798
from the *Description of Egypt*

FIG 10 BARON DOMINIQUE-VIVANT DENON
The Ruins of Hieraconpolis 1798–9
from the *Description of Egypt*

FIG 11 EDWARD WILLIAM LANE
View of the Pyramids 1826–7 from *Notes and Views in Egypt and Nubia*
(The British Library, London)

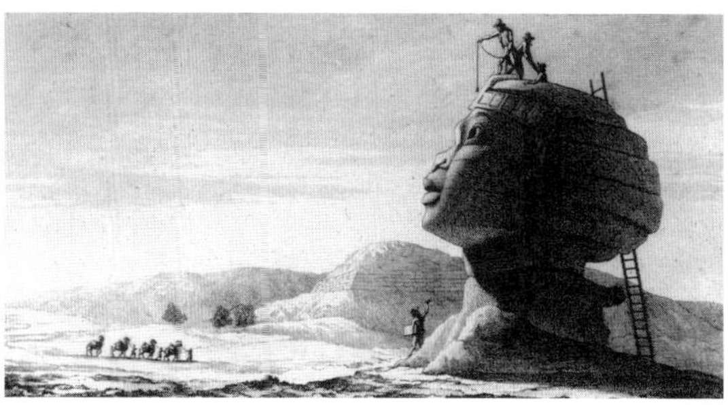

9

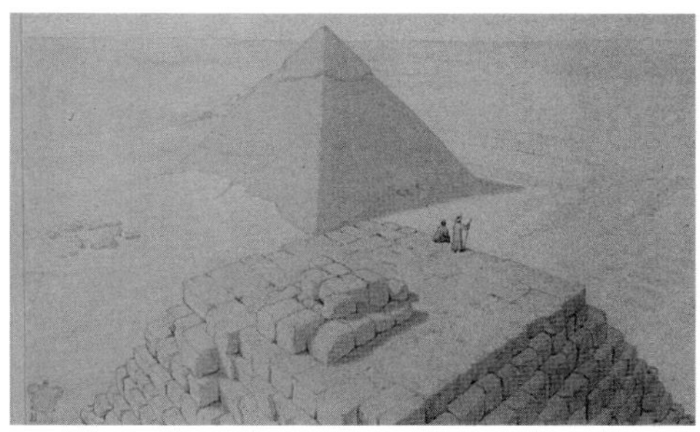

11

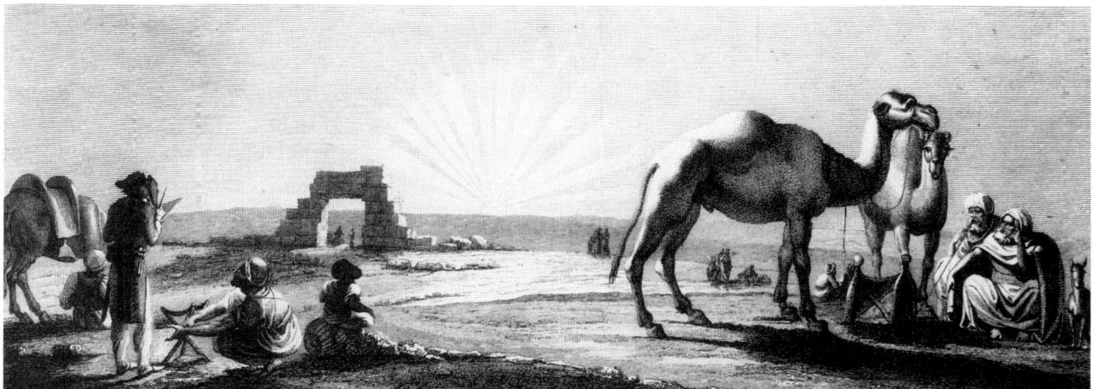

10

view. Here is a different approach from the intuitive and imaginative one of the Romantic sensibility. It denotes the desire for an objective and scientific way of seeing. Such determined efforts to eradicate error acknowledge a regrettable deficiency in our vision; we are all to a greater or lesser extent blind to the truth. Perhaps, they seem to say, if we can recover our sight, we can recover our memory, and regain what we have lost. The place to attempt this redemption is in desert places, among the stones of dead civilisations.

Further significant changes in attitude towards the Near East may be detected in the 1830s and 1840s. They are exemplified by the writing of the great Arabic scholar, Edward Lane, and the Scottish writer and historian, Thomas Carlyle. The publication of Lane's *Manners and Customs of the Modern Egyptians* in 1836 brought about an important advance in western perceptions and understanding of the Islamic East. Lane had spent years in the East, living like a Muslim gentleman, speaking Arabic and wearing Egyptian dress. What he was able to observe of Egypt is taken by Orientalists to be broadly representative of the Islamic Near East as a whole. Lane was also the translator of the *Arabian Nights* and the *Koran*, and the compiler of the first Arabic-English lexicon. Almost as influential, Carlyle gave a series of public lectures in 1840, that were subsequently published as *Heroes, Hero Worship and the Heroic in History*. His second lecture was entitled 'The Hero as Prophet. Mahomet: Islam', and in it Carlyle asserted the profound truths of Islam and the greatness of the Prophet.

A second generation of nineteenth-century writers and artists, students of the Near East who were originally inspired by fictional accounts, determined to go and see for themselves. The impelling spirit was that of the person who wants to check or verify an idea or sentiment. There is the seed of scepticism in this: mismatches between the imagined and the real would have to be acknowledged. This is the beginning of a change in perspective on the East.

SCOTTISH ORIENTALISTS

The three major Scottish painters who made the journey to the Near East in the nineteenth century, Sir William Allan, David Roberts and Sir David Wilkie, may be seen as representatives of different kinds of travellers. They also exemplify a gradual change from a 'Byronic Orientalism' towards one based on first-hand experience, an 'archaeological Orientalism'.

Sir William Allan 1782–1850

Allan travelled in Russia and Turkey between 1805 and 1814. His paintings of Oriental subjects are therefore to some extent based on actual observation. They are an admixture of reality and fantasy, combining carefully observed detail with heightened dramatic incident, rather after the manner of the *Arabian Nights*. His friend, Sir David Wilkie, recommended him to illustrate the *Arabian Nights* – perhaps in recognition of this character in his work. His treatment is essentially a continuation of the 'Byronic', but with all the trappings and authentic detail that give anecdotal conviction. That his experience in the East set him apart from other Scottish painters of the time was asserted by contemporaries.

Allan's admiration for Byron is apparent in several of his works. Not only did he paint subjects from Byron, such as *The Bride of Abydos*; he also commemorated the famous incident in the poet's life, the swimming of the Hellespont (fig 12). This incident exemplifies Byron's ability to dramatise, and virtually fictionalise, his own life. Allan, in turn, elaborated the incident, inventing the fisherman's lovely daughter in whose arms Byron recovers from his exertions.

Delight in theatricals and the collecting of curiosities marked Allan's attitude to the East. There is a description of a visit to Allan's studio by J. G. Lockhart:

... the most picturesque painting-room I fancy, in Europe ... The wainscoat is completely covered with rich clusters of military accoutrements, Turkish scimitars, Circassian bows and quivers ... interspersed with most gorgeous draperies of shawls, turbans, and saddle-cloths. Nothing can be more beautiful than the effect of the whole; and indeed I suppose it is, so far as it goes, a complete fac-simile of the barbaric magnificence of the interior decorations of an eastern palace. The exterior of the artist himself harmonized a good deal with his furniture; for he was arrayed, by way of robe-de-chambre, in a dark Circassian vest, the breast of which was loaded with innumerable quilted lurking-places, originally, no doubt, intended for weapons of warfare, but now occupied with the harmless shafts of hair-

pencils ... A swarthy complexion, and a profusion of black hair, tufted in a wild, though not ungraceful manner, together with a pair of large sparkling eyes, looking out from under strong shaggy brows, full of vivacious and ardent expressiveness – were scarcely less speaking witnessses of the life of roaming and romantic adventure, which, I was told, this fine artist had led.

Lockhart was struck by his manner, and in particular by the absence of something that could be called 'Scottishness'. Allan

... seemed to be full of a light and playful sportiveness, which is by no means common among the people of our nation, still less among the people of Scotland; and this again was, every now and then, exchanged for a depth of enthusiastic earnestness, still more evidently derived from a sojourn among men whose blood flows through their veins with a heat and a rapidity to which the North is a stranger.[27]

Lockhart comes close here to suggesting that the 'Romantic' temperament is an alien or untypical one in Scotland – a strange thing to say of the land of Macpherson and Scott. However, Scotland is, indeed, also the land of Smith and Hume. At any rate, if the values of utility and empiricism seemed somewhat oppressive in the middle of the nineteenth century, perhaps artists found here a reason to travel and to seek an alternative set of possibilities, and perhaps don a different personality.

Allan's pictures about slavery, such as *The Slave Market, Constantinople* (plate 6), contain echoes of Byron's political views in their criticism of the Ottoman Empire's assimilation of other nations. Interestingly, the latter painting also seems to contain the idea of an Orient made up of two opposing principles. The central incident is the cruel separation of the members of an enslaved family. The man is dragged off to the left, the dark side of the picture. The Circassian warrior on horseback has taken him into servitude. In contrast with the life of violence and action that awaits him, the woman's fate lies in the opposite direction; she will be taken to the harem. On the right-hand side of the picture all is indolence and inertia. The people, who represent different races of the Ottoman Empire, are impassive observers of the drama.

Here, Scott, who was a champion of Allan's, has a different basis for judgement from the one he had where Byron was the object of his approval. Whereas it was the economy of Byron's detail that was admirable, Allan's copiousness is striking. Studio props and Eastern paraphernalia have been accumulated in the presentation of a drama that impresses more in terms of spectacle than characterisation and plot. But, for Scott, whose visual acumen was notoriously idiosyncratic, 'a painting should, to be excellent, have something to say to the mind of a man, like myself, well-educated, and susceptible of those feelings which anything strongly recalling natural emotion is likely to inspire'. Painting, he said, should 'affect the human passions'.[28] When Allan came to paint Eastern subjects which were based in truth, like *A Circassian Chief*[29] (fig 13) or *Haslan Gheray crossing the Kuban,* they have all the hallmarks of Romantic fiction. The theatricality of their manner of presentation makes them look like literary inventions. *Haslan Gheray* is an illustration of a true story, published by Allan himself, of the abduction of a Circassian woman by a Crimean prince. The story is one that could have been the subject of a poem by Byron. This is a good instance of fact and fiction merging.

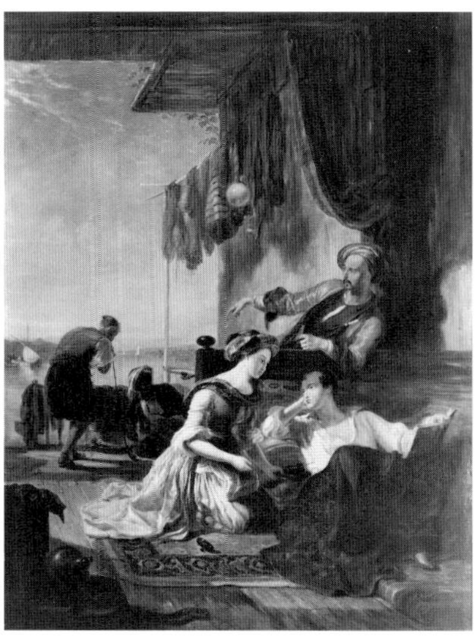

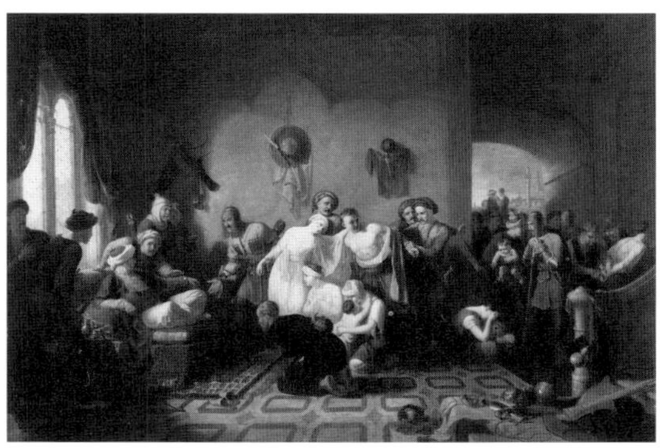

FIGS 12 & 13 SIR WILLIAM ALLAN

left *Lord Bryon Reposing in the House of a Turkish Fisherman, after having Swum across the Hellespont* 1830–1 (Location unknown)

above *A Circassian Chief Selling to a Turkish Pacha Captives of a Neighbouring Tribe Taken in War* 1815 (Earl of Wemyss and March)

David Roberts 1796–1864

David Roberts was a painter whose theatricality was deeper rooted than that of William Allan. In his youth, besides painting from imagination Eastern subjects, such as *The Israelites Leaving Egypt* (1827–9, fig 14), a work that invites comparison with the feverishly dramatic Biblical paintings of John Martin, Roberts worked as a painter of scenery and perspectival illusions for the stage.[30] However, a persuasive spectacle demanded accuracy, and Roberts determined upon a journey to the Near East. His biographer, Ballantine, wrote that, 'To visit the Holy Land, and make drawings of the scenes of sacred history and the antiquities of Egypt had been, long before the journey was undertaken by Mr Roberts, the brightest of his anticipations as an artist.'[31] This ambition was realised in 1838–9 when he undertook a journey up the Nile, and visited Sinai, Syria, Palestine and Lebanon.

Roberts travelled in order to give an authenticity and a foundation in observed reality to his representations of Eastern places and subjects. This is an archaeological approach to painting, taken further than that of painters such as Ingres, who relied for their researches upon secondary sources – book illustrations, eastern artefacts and accounts of travellers. It was the inadequacy of such sources that determined Roberts to go to the Near East. He knew the *Description de l'Égypte* by Denon, and considered the illustrations 'very incorrect'.[32] Whoever would make the journey to the East would greatly increase his store of visual material. However, the primary experience also promised more. One of the spurs to artists actually to travel was, no doubt, descriptions of the visual phenomena in the desert. Solid fact might be enriched by a strange new atmospheric fact. For example, Denon gave enticing descriptions of the colour changes that take place during a sand tornado:

This phenomenon, peculiar to these countries, would furnish the painter with effects and colouring entirely new. Everything that is usually pellucid, such as the sky, and the water, takes a gloomy opaque tint; all solid and hard bodies reflecting the few scattered rays which penetrate the cloud of dust, become brilliant, and have the appearance of transparency. The atmosphere assumes a yellow tint, changes the green of trees, and makes them appear blue; thus confusing the common order of nature; and reversing all its effects.[33]

Artists who read such descriptions must have been eager to see these astonishing natural phenomena for themselves. They opened up the possibility of painting entirely 'new' landscapes.

Occasionally, there is a painting by Roberts that combines actual experience and observation with a genuinely Romantic sensibility. *The Simoon* (fig 15) is one of these. This combination of actual conditions, colours and light effects – unique to the desert – marks an outstanding achievement in Roberts' s *oeuvre*. The picture treats one of the themes of Turner's late works: Nature as a cruel and destructive force. Man is burnt by the sun, his shelter and his works are crushed and swept away by the whirlwind. The painting recalls Denon's description above, and Roberts's ambition to depict such natural phenomena reflects Denon's observation that western painters would be excited by such effects because they had never been recorded in western art.

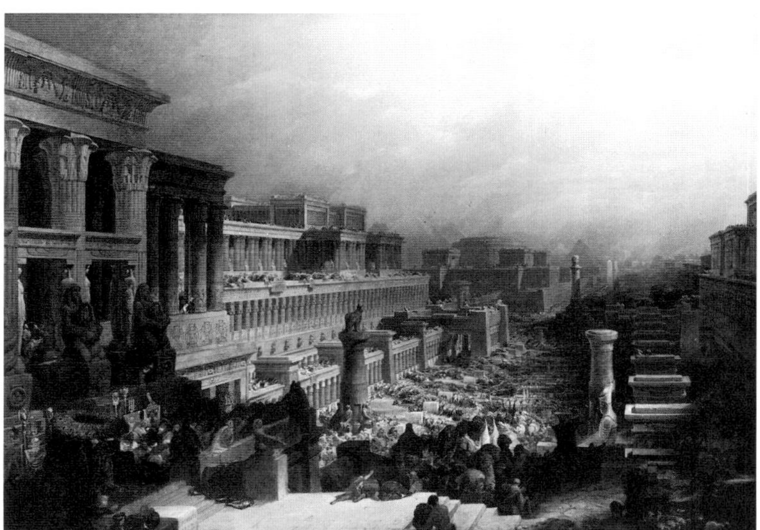

FIG 14 DAVID ROBERTS
The Israelites Leaving Egypt 1827–9
(Birmingham Museums and Art Gallery)

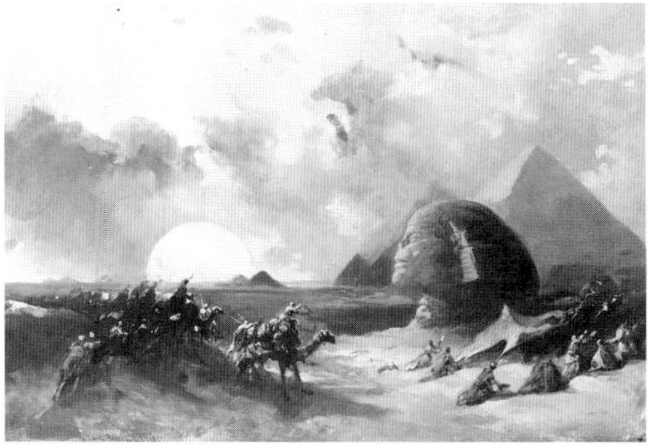

FIG 15 DAVID ROBERTS
The Simoon 1839 (Private Collection)

For the most part, however, Roberts's Eastern paintings are in the picturesque tradition, even, on occasion, reminiscent of landscapes by Claude, and Turner in his softer mood. It was, however, Roberts's general inability to attain the full measure of poetic expressiveness of Turner that prevented the critic John Ruskin from admiring him unreservedly. Roberts's journey east was to bring back the hard currency of material fact as well as the less negotiable credit of atmosphere, and he did not forget his first purpose. The inclusion of anecdotal detail and figure groups was criticised by Ruskin, in much the same terms that Scott had spoken of the redundancy of excessive detail in poetry. Ruskin complained of Roberts's Eastern pictures: 'We have been encumbered with caftans, pipes, scimitars ... when all that we wanted was a lizard, or an ibis.'[34] But the critic praised the spirit in which the works were done. They were, he said, 'the first studies ever made conscientiously by an English [*sic*] painter, not to exhibit his own skill, or make capital out of his subjects, but to give true portraiture of scenes of historical and religious interest. They were faithful and laborious beyond any outlines from nature I had ever seen.'[35]

Roberts's commitment to visual reality is tenacious in his drawings. Accuracy of detail was clearly of prime importance. In view of that fact, it is difficult to believe that he did not exploit artificial aids to drawing, in particular the camera lucida. He produced a prodigious number of drawings in the Near East, and they contain a vast amount of detail. All that can be said with certainty is that the instrument would have been very useful for speeding the work that he had in hand. He himself remarked upon his impressive output in his journal, but made no mention of mechanical or optical aids.[36] He would, in any case, have had to copy all details like hieroglyphics freehand. Artists often denied using the camera lucida, because it might be deemed by some to take away from their achievement. Roberts's drawings frequently have a curious mixture of tentativeness in the mark, sometimes a rather febrile, even shaky line, combined with an absolute certainty about the whereabouts of a mark in relation to others. This is characteristic of camera lucida drawings. So, evidence of style points to the use of the device, though firm proof is wanting.

Whilst the atmosphere of Roberts's pictures is occasionally of an 'alien' truthfulness, he generally favoured a certain Claudian tranquillity. The effect is to dislocate the scene from a sense of the present. Roberts often conveys admirably the sense that travellers in the Near East often described, of being in touch with the past. These places had not changed – or were in a process of change so much slower than that of the bustling modern world, and there was an often-expressed view that the people of the Near East had remained essentially the same since ancient times. Roberts was clearly drawn by these suggestions. In Egypt, the very monuments, emblematically the weather-worn Sphinx, bear witness to the inexorable ravages of time. In the spirit of the theatre, he attempts to persuade us of that pretended fact of the spectacle, that the interval of time that separates us from history has been done away with, and that we see the living pageant.

Roberts's response to the great monuments of ancient and past civilisations is not only documented in his art. After visiting Denderah, the subject of one of his most beautiful watercolours, he wrote in his journal:

I felt sad and solitary -not a soul but myself and my black guide within miles: all around was ... Desert ... the setting sun gilded the high peaks of the hills, throwing the shadow of the temples across the plain; and I reached my boat overcome by melancholy reflections on the mutability of all human greatness, and the perishable nature of even the most enduring works of human genius.[37]

The thought is by no means new. But it is eloquently expressed, and the paintings often have this elegiac mood. Claude is an appropriate model, for similar sentiments touch the wanderer in the Roman Campagna. Roberts sometimes achieves an unfamiliar and dreamlike atmosphere, for example, he paints Philae like a vision or a mirage (plates 7, 9). On occasion, too, Roberts was obliged by the subjects themselves to find unconventional ways of representing them. For example, to depict the temple at Baalbec (plate 8) he drew upon his experience as a theatrical scene painter to make a most daring and unexpected composition, creating dramatic spaces and a positively illusionistic spectacle.

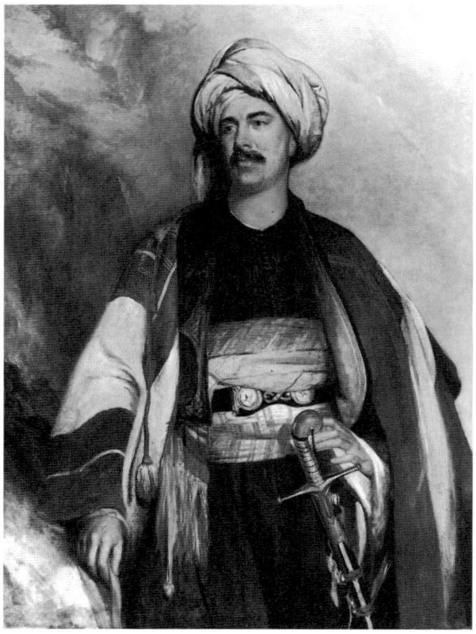

FIG 16 ROBERT SCOTT LAUDER
David Roberts 1840
(Scottish National Portrait Gallery, Edinburgh)

There was something of the actor evident in Roberts's adoption of eastern dress. He did so in order to disguise himself, with the specific purpose of entering mosques, and not to denote any empathy with, or attraction to, the eastern way of life.[38] He allowed himself, however, to be shown wearing eastern dress in the portrait made of him by Robert Scott Lauder (fig 16). As a result, Roberts becomes, in the painting, disguised indeed – very different from the unremarkable, bourgeois figure he presents in other portraits. As Baudelaire pointed out, the western suit and stiff collar is a costume that announces our ordinariness and that precludes the possibility of 'heroism' in everyday modern life. In Lauder's portrait, Roberts attains to a Romantic individuality that it was the very purpose of the 'uniform' of the western European male to deny. And with this spark of individualism, the Romantic fire was, however briefly and unexpectedly, kindled in Roberts on his eastern travels.

For Roberts, the experience of the East did not call in question the basic premises of his art. Despite his enthusiastic assumption of the garb of the East, he did not assimilate the deeper values of the place. The physical organ of sight remained fundamentally connected, by Western scientistic forms of explanation, to a single material reality. The poetic content of the work, as Roberts's journal confirms, rehearsed moods that the western sensibility was long accustomed to indulge.

Sir David Wilkie 1785–1841

Wilkie undertook his journey to the East the year after David Roberts, in 1840–1. After some time passed in Istanbul, he visited the Holy Land, moving on to Alexandria where he boarded the *Oriental* for the voyage home. He died on board ship, an event commemorated in Turner's great picture *Peace: Burial at Sea*. The sketches and few completed paintings done in the East are therefore Wilkie's last works.

The drawings in particular are notable for their strong and dramatic colours (plates 10–12). For a painter who often gave an 'old master' patina to his works, this is surprising. Whether they were preparatory sketches for works to be elaborated later, or spontaneous responses to scenes witnessed – a kind of visual travel journal recording 'the exuberance of paintable matter every day presents us with' – we do not know.[39] Nor can we know whether his style would have undergone any profound or permanent transformation as a result of his experience.

An important question in considering artists who encounter another culture and attempt to represent it is whether, released from their own social conventions, they are also released from the conventions of their art. What happens to an academic training when it is transported east, beyond the pale of European civilization? Wilkie was quite clear that the artist-traveller ought to see the place with different eyes from those of his mentors at the academy. For example, he wrote to the artist William Collins in 1837: *The impression that Rome has made upon you is not more than I expected ... As you are now in the prime of life, and at the height of your faculties and fame, why might not you, by the irresistable effort which a fresh theme inspires, form for yourself ... a new style of art; -what Claude, Poussin, Wilson, and Turner have owed to Italy, are advantages equally open to yourself? Your purpose of avoiding the beaten track of costumes, views, and imitations of others, the rock all young visitors split upon, is most judicious ...*[40]

Wilkie is a painter who had something of an assimilative or imitative habit. He had established a style based on the Dutch masters of the seventeenth century. His painting found a parallel between Lowland Scotland and the Protestant Low Countries – a natural sympathy of temperament and experience. But where he considered appropriate, he also looked to art elsewhere. Delacroix commented with amazement that Wilkie, whose work he admired, was, as a mature artist, open to the influences of Spanish painting.[41] In a similar way, Wilkie seems to have allowed his palette, his use of colour, to undergo the influence of the East, and perhaps also the arts of the East.[42]

This assimilative or emulative habit was constant in Wilkie. He stopped in Amsterdam on the way to Istanbul, and the effect was an immediate strengthening of the Rembrandtesque in his work – in, for example, the study for *The Turkish Letter-Writer* (fig 17). He also visited Cologne, where 'Rubens was again as great as ever'.[43] This openness to the influence of the art which he encountered makes it all the more probable that he was impressed, perhaps surprised and possibly affected by the indigenous arts of Turkey.

Wilkie took painting and sketching materials with him, but he also obtained materials in Istanbul.[44] A connection can be made, albeit not a 'necessary' one, between the materials of painting and the style. Is Wilkie's changed palette to be understood as more than a means of rendering a colourful scene – indeed as an attempt to achieve the style 'proper' to the place? Wilkie was a privileged visitor to Istanbul, having been granted a 'firman' or official pass by the sultan, that gained him admittance to the mosques and the palace of Topkapi.[45] He would, therefore, have seen the finest examples of Iznik tiles and decorative arts in Turkey. He may have encountered examples of Turkish miniatures. These were rare and almost exclusively housed in private libraries, but travellers might be privileged to see them.[46] If the miniature was considered as a traditional skill on a level with folk art or book illustration in the West, such an encounter would not have precluded general statements about the iconoclasm of the Turks and the absence of 'Art'.[47] There is an interesting cultural coincidence in that Turkish miniature painting, unlike Persian, was a realistic art: 'Turkish painting is descriptive and matter-of-fact and presents contemporary events in a direct, solemn and unemotional manner with ... a concern for psychological subtleties'. There is 'a modern tinge not otherwise found in the Islamic world: the strong interest in the lower classes, their economic life and their amusements'.[48]

One would expect the painter of *Distraining for Rent* and *Pitlessie Fair* to have had a certain empathy with such depictions.

Wilkie's stated purpose in travelling to the Near East was for the sake of an improved representation of Biblical subject-matter. The two paintings that were completed, *The Turkish Letter-Writer*[49] and *The Tartar Messenger Narrating the News of the Victory of St Jean d'Acre* (fig 18), have secular themes. The former reflects his observations about the condition of females in Turkish society.[50] Both paintings are about aspects of illiteracy, and social – even political – readings suggest themselves to the western viewer. In the case of *The Turkish Letter-Writer*, the themes of the subjugation of women and the constraints imposed by illiteracy seem to be set in parallel. When communication is uncertain because we have to rely upon others to convey messages for us, we cannot be in rational command. That is the social and philosophical dimension. The political corollary is the eventual danger of falling prey to misinformation, corruption and tyranny.

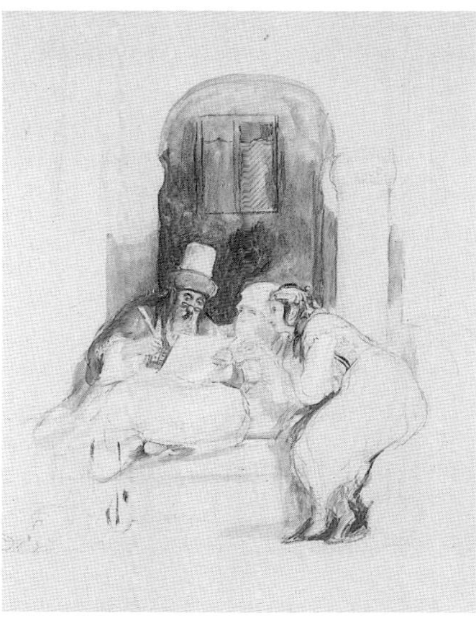

FIG 17 SIR DAVID WILKIE
Study for The Turkish Letter-Writer 1840
(Ashmolean Museum, Oxford)

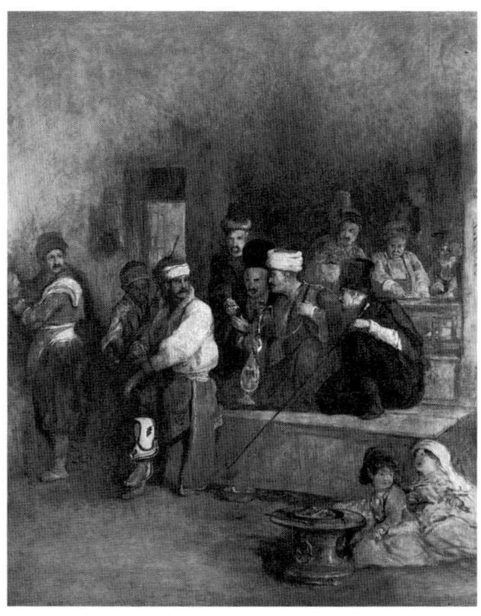

FIG 18 SIR DAVID WILKIE
The Tartar Messenger Narrating the News of the Victory of St Jean d'Acre 1840 (Private Collection)

The Tartar Messenger shows news of the victory of the Turkish and British over the rebellious Muhammad Ali of Egypt being brought to the patrons of a coffee shop. Wilkie had treated the same theme in *Chelsea Pensioners Receiving The London Gazette Extraordinary Announcing the Battle of Waterloo* (1822). The epic event is represented in its ramifications many miles from the battlefield or the parade ground, where actions in the Grand Manner are conducted. Wilkie chooses his 'performers' very much in the spirit of Rembrandt and of Calvinism. These are participants in good news, recounting the exploits of heroes but from a safe distance. Shakespeare had the same idea when, for example, he made Bardolph and his companions commentators on the action of *Henry V*.

Wilkie's attitude to the grander gestures of Romanticism was ambivalent. His early self-portrait has all the hallmarks and youthful intensity of an aspiring Romantic (fig 20). But perhaps he never entirely forgot the lesson of his early study of Dutch art of the seventeenth century, and especially of Rembrandt, that to 'plough one's own patch', to find subject-matter in everyday life and ordinary human experience, is a fitting and not ignoble aspiration for an artist. Wilkie was wryly sceptical of glamour and ideality and had a habit of debunking lofty Romanticism. For example, when, in Istanbul, his thoughts turned to Byron, it was not in a spirit of hero-worship. He noted in his journal:

Was shown the place in the Hellespont where Lord Byron swam across ... but in his transit, it is stated the noble poet was accompanied by a boat, which, if it takes away a little of the adventurous character of the effort, yet gives a little of that discretion his Lordship rather boasted of as being beneath his consideration.[51]

The authentic experience was central to Wilkie's thinking. Without it, invention could become 'hackneyed and unappreciated'. The idea of 'new food and fuel', the expression used by Wilkie when recommending William Allan to paint subjects from the *Arabian Nights*, is a suggestive one.[52] Evidently, the artist needs two kinds of energy. The food is the more prosaic: he should collect visual data. And he should find matter to fire his imagination. Secondary research could supply the former, but only travel itself could supply the latter, if the East was the subject. Travel enabled the art of the place to be matched with experience of the place. This empirical matter was to be shaped into an idea, and a painting of imaginative liveliness.

The idea of travelling in order to reinvigorate the creative faculties, to expose oneself to new influences and, most importantly, to discover means of escape from the conventionalities and clichés of an over-familiar art, these are not contradictory. For it is in art as much as life that alternatives and novelties are to be found. For all their differences, their journeying East represented for all three of these Scottish artists – Allan, Roberts and Wilkie – an escape, to some degree, from the stylistic and thematic conventions of western painting.

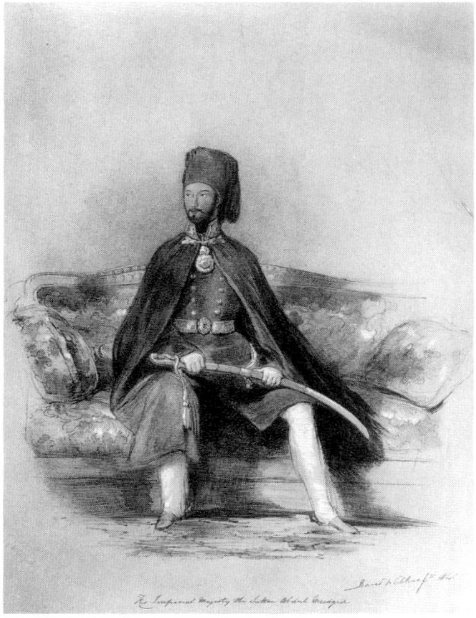

FIG 19 AFTER SIR DAVID WILKIE
His Imperial Majesty the Sultan Abdul Medgid 1840
(Victoria and Albert Museum, London)

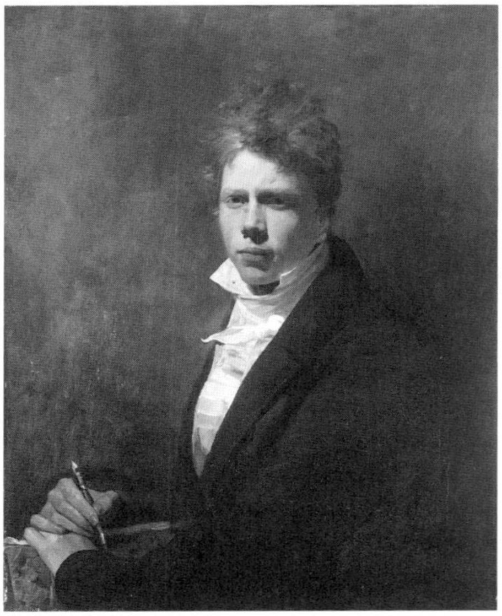

FIG 20 SIR DAVID WILKIE
Self-Portrait c.1804–5
(Scottish National Portrait Gallery, Edinburgh)

That a brief sojourn in the East should make such an impression on an artist's work as was the case so notably with Wilkie, prompts the question how much more would it do so in the case of artists who spent years in another country. John Frederick Lewis is an example of the long-time absentee. He departed on a tour of the Levant in 1840, possibly in emulation of Wilkie whom he greatly admired and whom he met in Istanbul in October that year.[53] Lewis was to live in Cairo for the following nine years. He adopted an Egyptian way of life, and when Thackeray saw him in 1844, he was 'living in the most Ottoman quarter of Cairo – in a house which might supply materials for half the Oriental annuals and manuals on Eastern architecture that appear in London and Paris'. He received the visitors who went to see him 'far away from the haunts of European civilisation ... in a long yellow gown ... curled up on the divan'.[54]

Dressing up and passing beyond the rationalist and positivist frame to where the true and the untrue are no longer opposites are acts of imagination and passion. They demand courage and seriousness. The comfort of a single perspective and, with it, of having a single and circumscribed existence is cast off. The sensitive traveller dresses up in the costume and, so far as he can, the mores of the people whom he visits. Unlike the traveller who continues, literally or metaphorically, to wear his frock coat and to bear his cultural burden on his back, the sensitive traveller aims at social invisibility, in order *not* to stand obdurately at his habitual perspective upon things. The vision that presents itself to this traveller to the East is one where strange, exciting and sometimes terrifying inversions of values occur. On occasion, the fact of such experiences can be used to contradict the certitudes of the West. At other times, they are for their own sake. A difference between the traveller who dresses up and the one who does not is that the former might decide not to go home.

Lewis was an artist who embraced the alternative possibilities that the East embodied. His life in the East was not necessarily that of Thackeray's 'languid lotus eater'. Certainly, that adopted by his friend, Edward Lane, the Orientalist scholar, was far from sybaritic. Rather, it emulated the well-regulated, disciplined Muslim way of life. Lane dressed in disguise in order to pass onto the other side of a barrier between people of different cultures and to gain insight and understanding. Lewis was play-acting too, but wanted to live, for a time, according to these different precepts, and to experience for himself the other life. He also worked very hard.

The work of J. F. Lewis reflects the influences of the art of the East (plates 13–17).[55] His paintings resemble Persian miniatures in their construction and spatial design. The colour is fresh and saturated. At the same time, though, the art of the West is never forgotten. Lewis's work was never so alien that he failed to satisfy his clientele at home.

His western artistic mentors were the great Venetian colourists; Rubens; Watteau and – among contemporaries – Delacroix.[56] John Ruskin praised his use of colour and even likened it to that of Veronese. When Lewis returned to Britain in the 1850s and exhibited his works, they were met with enthusiastic praise. And when he was criticised, it was for exemplifying values that were matter of topical debate; his work showed Pre-Raphaelite sympathies. The critic of *The Scotsman* in 1853, for example, saw in Lewis the 'painful distinctness ... an error of precisely the similar kind that begets many of the excesses of a Pre-Raphaelite ...'. Indeed, Lewis's pictures are hugely detailed. However, they should not be regarded as a sort of nineteenth-century 'reportage'. His 'realism' is a fiction, one created by the accumulation of detail. The details are accurately presented; the architectural settings, costumes, and concern for the rendering of atmosphere and light all give a heightened sense of truthful, observed reality. But the subjects – particularly when they represent the harem – are essentially imagined.

The harem pictures engage the observer by their hints at narrative interest. There is a certain subtlety of imagery and barely perceptible nuance of feeling or communication reminiscent of Vermeer and Chardin. Indeed, their frequently reticulated compositions also recall Vermeer. This echo of Dutch painting gave to his harem pictures a sub-tow of familiarity, and mitigated or veiled the erotic associations of the subject-matter. The apparently quiet domestic scenes, in which nothing much is going on, are a surface behind which we guess at discrete emotional and psychological dramas. But, if the choice is between meaning and surface, Lewis seems to be more interested in the latter. It is the optical rather than the inner truth that counts more.

The surfaces, often geometrically patterned, receive a care in execution that is relentless. The observer performs a more or less unconscious computation of time spent by the painter, and often finds a figure upstaged by a hanging or inlaid panel. But this is not all. Lewis's works are distinctive because of his use of light and the omnipresent lattice. He makes indoor scenes that are suffused with the outdoors. Or, he depicts courtyards that are out of doors, yet a part of an intensely private, insular existence. Light penetrates and permeates: it discloses forms and colours, and simultaneously dissolves and dissipates. It renders figures transient and almost intangible – like a mirage or a dream. The women of the harem thus become visions – creations of the artist's imagination.

Ruskin, the defender of the Pre-Raphaelite painters, considered *A Frank Encampment on the Desert of Mount Sinai* (fig 21) 'among the most *wonderful* pictures in the world'.[57] He described it as 'a portrayal of harmony between East and West, a vision of the Levant as a *fête champêtre*, and a commentary on the immutability of eastern desert life'. The three themes discerned here would serve to describe the essential character of Lewis's Orientalist art. Particularly important is the intuition of a spiritual allegiance with Watteau: the Levant as *feté champêtre*. Lewis had made copies of paintings by Watteau, including the *Embarkation for the Island of Cythera*.[58] The key is lighter, the labour is differently distributed and the curves of *rocaille* give way to the straight edge, but Lewis's work, in its concern with the female perspective, and in its veils and screens and patterns, holds something of the spirit of such paintings by Watteau.

Another English artist, Frederick Leighton, found a kind of purity and asceticism in the very opulence and beauty of the arts of the Orient. His London home, Leighton House in Holland Park, performs a remarkable homage to the arts of the East. It has the coolness of turquoise tiles; a fountain plays; verses from The Koran are inscribed around the frieze, and all serve to counteract the materialism of the typical Victorian interior. There is an unexpectedly monastic ambience in this cool domain where the luxury of the East is suggested. If this chaste pavilion was ever populated with a harem it would have consisted of remote goddesses, women like those of Leighton's own creation. There is perhaps a paradox at the heart of Islamic art. Nothing could more delight the senses, but nothing is more refined and serene in its abstraction.

Leighton's own Oriental pictures are a curious mixture of minutely observed and carefully recreated settings (often assembled with the aid of photographs), and a western figure style. This fusion of eastern setting and western tradition is most successful in works such as *Old Damascus* (1873–4, plate 22). It is the setting, with its precisely rendered architectural features that tell us that the scene is set in the Near East and not fourteenth-century Italy. The painting has a purity of design and mood that reflects Leighton's association with the Nazarene artists. In general, the finished paintings compare unfavourably with the oil sketches, which anticipate Impressionism in their freshness of colour and immediacy of vision. These qualities could be curiously compromised in a painting that was 'finished' and submitted for public approval. *Portion of the Interior of the Grand Mosque of Damascus* (1873–5, plate 23) is painted with the academic flair at which Leighton was so brilliant, and yet includes the foreground woman and child who, despite their

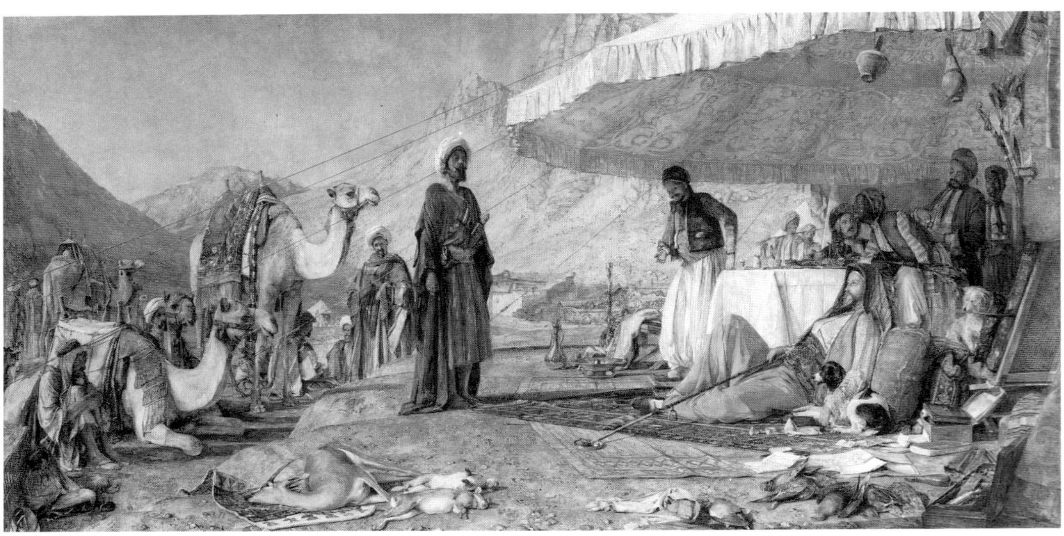

FIG 21 JOHN FREDERICK LEWIS
A Frank Encampment on the Desert of Mount Sinai 1842
(Yale Center for British Art, New Haven)

eastern dress, are treated in a somewhat anecdotal manner. Their actions and purpose in the painting are unclear, and their redundancy to the more serious activity that has become their backdrop makes them seem dislocated from their surroundings, resembling in this nothing so much as western sightseers. Because Leighton's Orientalist works include so many characteristics of British art of the period, and reflect contemporary taste, they become inexorably 'Victorian'. They are victims of a kind of anachronistic gloss that art can impose upon life.

Another academic painter who treated an eastern subject in one of his major works was Sir Edward Poynter. Poynter's *Israel in Egypt* (1867, plate 24) is an example of the way in which eastern themes could be accommodated to western artistic requirements and norms. Poynter makes out of the fantastic recreation of the splendours of the monuments of Ancient Egypt the background for an elaborate spectacle that questions the nature of human glory that depends upon the subjugation of slaves. Samuel Johnson had written in *The History of Rasselas* that the pyramids were:

a monument of the insufficiency of human enjoyments. A king whose power is unlimited ... is compelled to solace, by the erection of a pyramid, the satiety of dominion and tastelessness of pleasures, and to amuse the tediousness of declining life, by seeing thousands labouring without end, and one stone, for no purpose, laid upon another. Whoever thou art, not content with a moderate condition ... survey the pyramids, and confess thy folly![59]

THE ORIENT OF FACT

That artists were travelling partly in order to find new subjects and new possibilities – colouristic and even stylistic – for their work seems universally applicable. The most important and often stated reason for the journey east was for the sake of a reinvigoration of the painting of Scriptural subjects. While it was the avowed and, doubtless, the prime reason, in the case of Hunt, Seddon, Wilkie and Roberts, that they wanted to give an authority and veracity to their religious paintings, they can seem to have been driven by a rather dreary sense of duty. On the other hand, while the East made possible formal change and a fresh vision, the call of veracity could seem alluring and seductive. It is noticeable that the colour in the work of the majority of the artists undergoes some essential change.

Holman Hunt refers to duty and pleasure in his letter of 1850, from Jerusalem, to Dante Gabriel Rossetti:

I am not satisfied with the thousand books of travel that come out every year; but even these in all their trivialities and superficialities are a keen reproof to painters. I have a notion that painters should go out ... like merchants of nature, and bring back precious merchandise in faithful pictures of scenes interesting from historical consideration or from the strangeness of the subject itself.[60]

This gives an insight into Hunt's wider intention. The desire to paint authentic and original religious subjects may be the most important driving motive, but there was more. The fact that he can allow the fascination of the subject for its own sake is significant and surprising, for it anticipates *aestheticism.*

As a Pre-Raphaelite, Hunt was already a committed anti-academic painter. He believed in the need to revitalise art by freeing it from conventional restraints. A new, vernacular language for painting was needed that would be capable of direct communication and that would replace the dead language of Classicism. An evangelical Christianity could make a similar criticism of institutional Christianity. While his particular commitment was to a moral and religious school of painting, he went to the East because he believed that an escape from convention was possible there. He had noted that the drawings done in the Near East by archaeological draughtsmen such as Robert Kerr Porter and Joseph Bonomi, while 'uninspiring', nonetheless represented 'a truthful way of approaching the East, seemingly unencumbered by artistic conventions'.[61] Hunt's own paintings done in the Holy Land are characterised by a zealous commitment to the idea of truth to nature (plates 18, 19).

Hunt's reluctance to adopt Arab dress in the Holy Land is emblematic of his refusal to enter into a sympathetic, receptive state of mind.[62] He obdurately refused to see from another perspective because of profound opposition both to the values of an alien culture and to the possibility of having his own certainties questioned. While he shared the Romantics' belief that conventions stood in the way of vision, feeling and understanding, he was fundamentally hostile to the Romantic spirit in art. His was a purposive enterprise – not to be sidetracked or distracted by Romantic sentiments. He wore the costume back home, however, where it was clearly a sign to others that he had made the arduous pilgrimage: he had gained his Orientalist credentials.

Thomas Seddon joined Hunt in the Holy Land in 1854. The few paintings done there demonstrate his absolute commitment to painting from nature. His most extraordinary work, *The Valley of Jehoshaphat,* was painted 'to present to those who could not visit it themselves an accurate record, not a fancy view, of the very ground our Saviour so often trod' (plate 20).[63] It showed the Garden of Gethsemane and the Mount of Olives, places of particular significance associated with the last days of Christ's life.

The painter who abandoned formulae and conventions for the sake of rigorous topographical accuracy had chosen the arduous path. Hunt pointed out to Seddon the pitfalls that lay before the artist who as, it, were followed John the Baptist in untrodden territory. 'It was scarcely in the pictorial sense a landscape,' he wrote. He continued:

... in conventional art the demand for variety of tones was satisfied by exaggeration and tricks, and ... these had increased the due expectation for effect to such an extent that when a work was done strictly from Nature, unless all the variety that Nature gave was rendered by the painter, the spectator had good cause for declaring the work crude and false.[64]

Most commentators were somewhat bewildered by the resulting work. John Ruskin, more perceptive and sympathetic than most, wrote of Seddon's paintings that they were the first 'truly historic landscape art: that is to say they are the first landscapes uniting perfect artistical skill with topographic accuracy being directed with stern self-restraint to no other purpose than that of giving to persons who cannot travel ... the perfect sensation of its reality wholly unmodified by the artist's execution'.[65]

Hunt had not exactly solved the problems of working from Nature himself, and Ruskin was to find fault with his painting of *The Scapegoat* (fig 22) Hunt had painted 'crag by crag, the purple mountains of Moab, and grain by grain, the pale ashes of

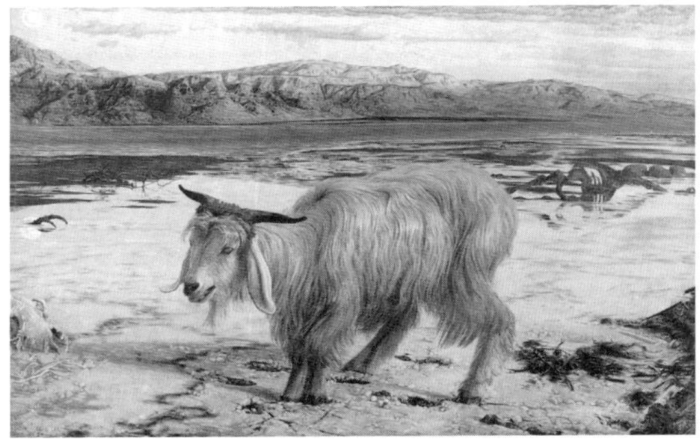

FIG 22 WILLIAM HOLMAN HUNT
The Scapegoat 1854 (Walker Art Gallery, Liverpool)

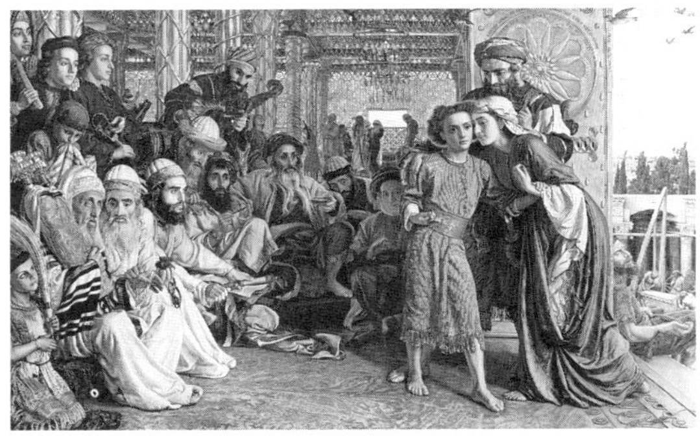

FIG 23 WILLIAM HOLMAN HUNT
The Finding of the Saviour in the Temple 1854–5 (Walker Art Gallery, Liverpool)

Gomorrah ... but it is not *good* painting'.[66]

It is interesting, in this context, to note that Seddon and Hunt employed photographs of the Holy Land in order to help them finish paintings after their return to Britain. That is, photographs were used purely as accurate recordings providing useful visual information. Hunt and Seddon exemplify the extremes of commitment to an objective visual description. Their use of the camera is virtually the same as previous artists' use of the camera lucida – that is, as an objective and mechanical means of seeing.

The colours found in the eastern paintings of Hunt and Seddon are unlike those in other landscapes. They recall Denon's description of bizarre colour effects in the desert. There is little doubt, given the commitment of these artists to the truth of observation, that the unfamiliar, and sometimes lurid, colour effects in Hunt and Seddon are based on actual observation.

Another painter who worked with the most minute fastidiousness was Edward Lear. He too treated geological fact and, by a process of almost microscopic description, created effects that we sometimes think belong in the display-cabinet and are sometimes persuaded show the very colours of the East. However, *The Pyramids Road, Gizeh* of 1873 (plate 21) is somewhat unusual. It is a populous picture. It shows a bifurcation: a tunnel of trees along which moves modern Egypt, and, in the immeasurable distance, the ancient pyramids at Gizeh. The device of using the pallor of aerial perspective to signify a ghostly presence was developed most intently by Turner. Lear gratefully receives Turner's suggestion. Hunt, on the other hand, does something surprising, if not unprecedented, in his picture of the Sphinx, for he adopts a point of view as close as possible to the emblem of the ghost and the enigma and turns it into geological strata (plate 19). By painting the back view of the monument, he actually suggests that we are effectively seeing from the Sphinx's point of view – not an experience of space, but one of time.

The strangeness of Holman Hunt's works, painted or conceived in the Near East, is a result of his single-minded dedication to the curious notion of making Biblical events 'tangible' – a phrase used by Hunt of his painting *The Finding of the Saviour in the Temple* (fig 23) This was laboriously painted with an anthropological exactitude that equalled the topographical and zoological determination of *The Scapegoat.* This literal-minded obsession with visual facts, although high-minded and doubtless intended to create paintings resonant with poetry, ultimately led to the most prosaic of religious works: 'omens', as Ruskin said, rather than 'achievements'.[67]

A FRENCH TRAVELLER

The 'East imagined' and the 'East observed' have so far been considered separately. Florid imaginings and confusing realities have not mixed. But in one writer in particular, the strongest power of imagination is at one with the most acute powers of perception. The French writer, Gustave Flaubert, is artist-traveller of the mid-nineteenth century *par excellence.* Flaubert travelled to the Near East at a time (1849–50) when he had lost his sense of artistic direction. Uncertain of his own identity as an artist, he was suffering from a curious 'modern' malady – an inability to decide what his subject-matter should be. Flaubert had an irreverent and cynical attitude to the business of fact-gathering upon which he and the journalist and photographer, Maxime Du Camp, were engaged by the French government. He did not take his remit seriously, but, on the contrary, idly drank in the experiences and contemplated his artistic career:

When I think of my future (that happens rarely, for I generally think of nothing at all despite the elevated thoughts one should have in the presence of ruins!) ... I am full of doubt and indecision ...[68]

Flaubert combined cynicism with an interest in the most sordid and earthy reality. The contradiction on the one hand contends with, and on the other hand disguises, a hypersensitive and fragile temperament.[69] In the Near East, he sought out and explored the exotic and sensual, and described his encounters clinically and with graphic detail, in much the same way as Maxime Du Camp, his travelling companion, sought the inscriptions on ancient monuments and made casts and photographs of them.

The ostensible search for 'truth' about the past is a facet of Romanticism. Science and art, art and archaeology are not antithetical within the Romantic spirit. The amateur archaeologists Dawkins and Wood were depicted by Gavin Hamilton, amid the ruins of Palmyra, wearing Classical togas. Byron wrote about Sardanapalus within the restrictions of a self-imposed discipline, the Classical unities. Ingres recreated a Classical mythology in the archaeological settings for his most complete expressions of eastern sensuality, the odalisques. Flaubert would write the novel *Madame Bovary,* about a contemporary bourgeoise provincial woman, which is a re-statement of the essential Orientalist theme: the desire to escape from a life of small-minded ambition and an irksome and pedestrian reality. Emma Bovary dreams of living outwith the petty restrictions and conventions of real life, and inhabiting a world where there was no contradiction between delighting the senses and a life of virtue. Her tragedy is that she mistakes the fiction for a real possibility. She thought the Isle of Cythera was a real place. The myth destroyed her. With bitter irony, Flaubert gives her a place in the novel that is restrictive, like the harem. The novel was written after Flaubert's return from Egypt. There is a story told by Du Camp:

On the Borders of Lower Nubia, on the summit of Gebel Abusir, which overlooks the Second Cataract, as we were watching the Nile dash itself against the sharp black granite rocks, he [Flaubert] gave a cry: 'I have found it! Eureka! Eureka! I will call her Emma Bovary! [70]

It has been suggested that the story is apocryphal. Yet, that the central idea of the novel should have emerged from this experience in the Middle East, makes perfect sense. Emma Bovary read Oriental novels, and Frédéric in *L'Education Sentimentale* collected prints of exotic places, including Istanbul. A few days before he died, almost thirty years after the eastern journey, Flaubert was 'gripped by the longing to see a palm tree standing out against the blue sky, and to hear a stork clacking its beak at the top of a minaret'.[71]

Flaubert may be regarded as a 'spokesman' for western travellers in the mid-nineteenth century. In his travel journals and letters, he gave uncommon expression to common experiences. In his *Notes de Voyage*, for example, Flaubert described the 'initial bedazzlement' of arriving in Egypt:

It is like being hurled while still asleep into the midst of a Beethoven symphony, with the brasses at their most ear-splitting, the bases rumbling, and the flutes sighing away; each detail reaches out to grip you; it pinches you; and the more you concentrate on it the less you grasp the whole. Then gradually all this becomes harmonious and the pieces fall into place of themselves, in accordance with the laws of perspective. But the first days, by God, it is such a bewildering chaos of colours that your poor imagination is dazzled as though by continuous fireworks as you go about staring at minarets thick with white storks, at tired slaves stretched out in the sun ... at the patterns of sycamore branches against walls, with camel bells ringing in your ears and great herds of black goats bleating in the streets amid the horses and the donkeys and the pedlars ... You brush against all the costumes of the Orient, elbow all its peoples ...[72]

Flaubert also expresses a common experience of western travellers in the Near East: that of thinking they had been there before: *You ask me whether the Orient is up to what I imagined it to be. Yes, it is; and more than that, it extends far beyond the narrow idea I had of it. I have found, clearly delineated, everything that was hazy in my mind. Facts have taken the place of suppositions -so excellently so that it is often as though I were suddenly coming upon old forgotten dreams.*[73]

His expectations were realised:

Anyone who is a little attentive rediscovers here much more than he discovers. The seeds of a thousand notions that one carried within oneself grow and become more definite, like so many refreshed memories. Thus, as I landed at Alexandria I saw before me, alive, the anatomy of the Egyptian sculptures ... The dances that we have had performed for us are of too hieratic a character not to have come from the dances of the old Orient, which is always young because nothing changes. Here the Bible is a picture of life today ... [74]

Later on, he recognised, in the dancing of the almehs, something he really had seen before – on Greek vases. If, however, making sense of his experiences in the Orient by linking fact with fiction and reality with representations of it, he was not prepared for many of the things which, unanticipated, took him by surprise. He described the colour and light effects which he had never encountered before:

Sunset over Medinet Habu. The mountains are dark indigo ... blue over dark grey, with contrasting horizontal stripes of purplish red in the clefts of the valleys. The palms are black as ink, the sky is red, the Nile has the look of molten steel.[75]

These new sights prompted unrehearsed emotions. It was while contemplating this scene, and listening to the sailors on the boat, playing their music, that Flaubert had a significant experience:

... as I was enjoying those things, and just as I was watching three wave-crests bending under the wind behind us, I felt a surge of solemn happiness that reached out towards what I was seeing, and I thanked God in my heart for having made me capable of such joy: I felt fortunate at the thought, and yet it seemed to me that I was thinking of nothing: it was a sensuous pleasure that pervaded my entire being.[76]

The momentary pure enjoyment of a complete gratification of the senses, and the experience of it as a spiritual, almost a mystical one, is a recurring theme of Orientalist art. One of Flaubert's most significant experiences was the night spent with a 'famous courtesan', known as Kuchuk Hanem. He described the encounter, with the detail of a physician, in letters to friends, and assuaged the anger of his mistress, Louise Colet, on the subject by observing of Kuchuk:

You and I are thinking of her, but she is certainly not thinking of us. We are weaving an aesthetic around her, whereas this particular very interesting tourist who was vouchsafed the honours of her couch has vanished from her memory completely, like many others. Ah! Travelling makes one modest – you see what a tiny place you occupy in the world.[77]

Flaubert is not thinking exclusively of Kuchuk here either. He has deliberately created a simile that would apply to the larger matter – the nature of the westerner's encounter with the East. No matter how profoundly affected by the experience, the westerner has not touched the object of his fascination. The East, asserts Flaubert, sphinx-like and too ancient to be affected, is ultimately impervious and indifferent to the travellers from the West. The traveller, then, is transfigured by this thought into a wraith or a ghost – and the end of the Romantic journey is reached, an existence outside matter, through a plunge into the world of sense.

While it has been discussed in terms of the tenets of Romanticism, Orientalism – in the sense of a fascination with the mythology of the East either as 'desert' or 'oasis' – is a recurring theme in western art. Traditionally and metaphorically for the West, the desert represents a place where, surrounded by emptiness and in solitude, the true 'self' may be discovered.[78] In the oasis, the westerner rediscovers the life of the senses. As well as an exercise in cultural studies, western travel has had an existential pretext. Byron's Childe Harold attempts to rid himself of his past, and by implication, to leave the old 'self' behind, by going to the desert. Artists like Holman Hunt whose 'Orientalism' was conceived in a spirit of utilitarian and archaeological piety rather than Byronic egotism, had, by their forensic examination of the physical realities of the Near East, effectively negated it as a retreat for the imagination. By the end of the nineteenth century, the East of Byron and of Hunt had both ceased to be credible. The journey that used to be to the East, at least potentially, changed its goal. The place of self-discovery, or where the shadows and heat and luxury of the harem could be recreated, came to be the internal terrain, the individual imagination.

The seeds of decadence were present in Byron's *Turkish Tales*. Hazlitt was writing a critique of Byron in 1825, when news of the poet's death in Greece arrived to silence him. He had already written this telling passage:

Lord Byron's earlier productions, Lara, The Corsair, &c. were wild and gloomy romances, put into rapid and shining verse. They discover the madness of poetry, together with the inspiration: sullen, moody, capricious, fierce, gloating on beauty, thirsting for revenge, hurrying from the extremes of leisure to pain, but with nothing permanent, nothing healthy or natural. The gaudy decorations of the morbid sentiments remind one of flowers strewed over the face of death![79]

The recognition of the affinity between the spirit of Byron's poetry and that of the 'Divine Marquis' (de Sade) is implicit.[80] Later in the nineteenth century, the Sardanapalus of Delacroix would have his female counterparts in Flaubert's Queen of Sheba, Swinburne's Cleopatra, and the basilisk Salomes of Gustave Moreau and Oscar Wilde. What Mario Praz described as the 'fury of frenzied action' characteristic of Romanticism gave way to the 'sterile contemplation' of Decadence.[81]

The chain that links the two is the spirit of Orientalist art through its gradual metamorphosis and absorption into the exoticism that is, by definition, recreated and experienced alone – in an environment of one's own making – in darkened rooms. *Fin de siècle* ennui is an experience of satiety, metaphorically upon a litter of cushions, cooled by a peacock-feather fan. When the curtains are drawn upon the busy world, imagination can conjure spirits out of the shadows, indulge the most dangerous fantasies, explore without restraint the life of the senses. This was the life chosen by Huysmans's character, Des Esseintes, in *A Rebours.* He is the emblematic figure of the age of Decadence. But his are bitter pleasures, for they find no confirmation in external reality. The imagined Orient had been lost irretrievably.

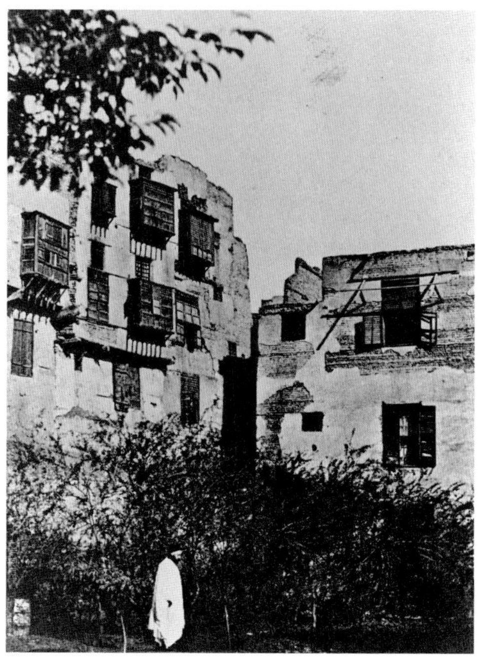

FIG 24 MAXIME DU CAMP
Flaubert in the Garden of the Hôtel du Nil, Cairo 1850
(Victoria and Albert Museum, London)

Notes and References

1 Edmond & Jules de Goncourt, *French Eighteenth-Century Painters*, Oxford, 1981, p.7.

2 Edward Said, *Orientalism*, London, 1991.

3 Variously titled: *The Thousand and One Nights*, and *The Arabian Nights Entertainments*, this is usually referred to by the abbreviated title the *Arabian Nights*.

4 Leila Ahmed, *Edward W. Lane: A study of his life and works and of British ideas of the Middle East in the nineteenth century*, London & New York, 1978, pp.133–4.

5 *The Bride of Abydos, The Corsair, The Giaour* (1813) and *Lara* (1814).

6 *Byron, A Self-Portrait: Letters and Diaries 1798 to 1824*, ed. Peter Quennell, Oxford, 1990, p.231.

7 Letter to Thomas Moore, 30 Nov. 1813, op.cit., p.201.

8 Francis Jeffrey, for his unsigned review of *Childe Harold's Pilgrimage*, Canto III, *Edinburgh Review*, 1816–17. This was the same Jeffrey that Byron had savaged in his *English Bards and Scotch Reviewers* of 1809.

9 Samuel Johnson, *The History of Rasselas, Prince of Abyssinia*, 1759.

10 George Gordon, Lord Byron, 'Notes to Childe Harold's Pilgrimage', *The Poetical Works*, London, 1960, p.884.

11 He referred to the Greeks, with customary irony, as 'a kind of eastern Irish papists' and asked, rhetorically, '… shall we then emancipate our Irish Helots? Mahomet forbid!' ibid.

12 'The Arnaouts, or Albanese, struck me forcibly by their resemblance to the Highlanders of Scotland, in dress, figure, and manner of living. Their very mountains seemed Caledonian, with a kinder climate. The kilt, though white; the spare, active form; their dialect, Celtic in its sound, and their hardy habits, all carried me back to Morven. No nation are so detested and dreaded by their neighbours as the Albanese.' op.cit.,1960, pp.876–7.

13 Scott, letter to J.B.S. Morritt, 4 May 1812. Quoted in *Byron: The Critical Heritage*, ed. Andrew Rutherford, London, 1970, p.37.

14 Scott, *Quarterly Review*, Feb. 1817, ibid., p.91.

15 Loc.cit., p.90.

16 10 July 1817, op.cit., 1990, p.412.

17 See note 13, pp.88–9.

18 Byron, 1960, p.252.

19 Description by Baron Rivet, the first owner of the sketch. Quoted by Lee Johnson, *The Paintings of Delacroix: A Critical Catalogue*, Oxford, 1981, p.114.

20 It is ironic that the least 'Byronic' of Byron's works, the one in which he exercised great restraint and even worked within the Classical rules of decorum (dismissing violence from the stage etc.) should have triggered such an explosion of violence and colour in the painter's imagination.

21 If we will imaginatively adopt the perspective of the victim at the foot of the bed an instant earlier, we will see a gesture by Sardanapalus that recalls that of God in Michelangelo's *Last Judgement*. The irony compounds the shocking nature of the scene.

22 *Flaubert in Egypt*, ed. & trans. Francis Steegmuller, London, 1972, p.214.

23 *The Travel Letters of Lady Mary Wortley Montagu*, ed. A.W. Lawrence, London, 1930, p.198.

24 Ibid. pp.148–9.

25 Edward Said says that Napoleon turned Egypt into 'a department of French learning' in which 'everything said, seen, and studied was to be recorded, and indeed was recorded in that great collective appropriation of one country by another, the *Description de l'Égypte…*'. op.cit. pp.84–5.

26 *Voyage dans la Basse et la Haute Égypte, pendant les Campagnes du Générale Bonaparte* (1802); *Description de l'Égypte, ou Recueil des observations et des recherches qui ont été faits in Égypte pendant l'expédition de l'armée francaise, publié par les ordres de sa majesté l'empéreur Napoléon le grand*, 23 vols, Paris, 1808–29.

27 John Gibson Lockhart, *Peter's Letters to his Kinsfolk*, ed. William Ruddick, Edinburgh, 1977, pp.116–17.

28 Sir Walter Scott, *The Journal*, Edinburgh, 1927, pp.118–19, entry for 13 Feb. 1826.

29 This painting, which was exhibited at the Royal Academy in 1816 was thought to have been lost. It would seem to be the picture, also known as *The Circassians*, which was won by the Earl of Wemyss in a lottery organised by Sir Walter Scott and others. The painting in the Wemyss collection has the fuller title inscribed on the back.

30 In 1829, he was making 'dioramic views' for the Queen's Bazaar in Oxford Street, London, and painting 'views representing the march of the Grand Russian Army into Turkey' for the Christmas Pantomime at Covent Garden.

31 James Ballantine, *The Life of David Roberts* RA, Edinburgh, 1866, p.231.

32 Kenneth Bendiner, 'David Roberts in the Near East: social and religious themes', *Art History*, vol.6, no.1, March 1983, p.79.

33 Baron Dominique-Vivant Denon, *Egypt Delineated*, 1825, p.220.

34 *The Works of John Ruskin*, ed. E. T. Cook & A. Wedderburn, vol.III, London, 1903–12, p.223. Roberts was impervious to the criticism of Ruskin as he was to his rhetoric in *Modern Painters*. The painter Frederick Goodall wrote: 'I have never forgotten what he [Roberts] said at the time when Ruskin was urging young artists to paint grass, and opening flowers, and the pebbles on the sea-shore… "It is to me a maist melancholy thing to see a young artist fancying he is makin' himself a penter by sitting for sax months in front o' a grozet (gooseberry) buss".' *The Reminiscences of Frederick Goodall* RA, London, 1902, p.225.

35 John Ruskin, *Praeterita*, Oxford,1979, p.237. Ruskin was referring to Roberts's watercolours which he had seen exhibited in the spring of 1840. He was not an admirer of the lithographs by Louis Haghe that were subsequently published. Ruskin would have been particularly aware of the superiority of Roberts over his predecessors in the field. He wrote that: 'The endeavours at representation of Oriental character or costume which accompany the travels of even the best educated English traveller either during or immediately after the Peninsula War, are without exception the clumsiest, most vulgar, and most ludicrous pieces of work that ever disgraced draughtsmen, savage or civil.'

36 Of his drawings of Egyptian temples, he wrote, 'I may not have done them justice, but few artists of my standing could afford more time, and I daresay, few could have produced more in the same number of days.' Ballantine, op.cit.,p.99.

37 Ibid., p.89.

38 Roberts's journals are peppered with disparaging references to the Eastern religion and way of life.

39 Allan Cunningham, *Life of Sir David Wilkie*, London,1843, vol.III, p.338.

40 Cunningham, vol.III, pp.219–20.

41 Op.cit., vol.III, p.513 : '...when he visited Spain he contended that Velasquez was the wisest of all great colourists; and, without exactly imitating him, mixed his palette under his influence.' Delacroix wrote: 'He [Wilkie] came to see me and to show me a few drawings he had just brought back from an extensive journey in Spain. He seemed to me entirely overwhelmed by the pictures he had seen there: I marvelled that a man of such genuine genius, on the verge of old age, could be influenced to such an extent by works so very unlike his own.' (Letter to Théophile Silvestre, 31 Dec.1858.) *Eugène Delacroix: Selected Letters, 1813–1863*, trans. J. Stewart, London, 1971, p.352.

42 It may be more than coincidental that the use of strong and uncompromising reds that emerge out of a darker, monochrome background which is characteristic of Wilkie's eastern drawings, is reminiscent of much of Delacroix's practice. There was certainly a mutual admiration between them, and that there may have been some kind of stylistic cross-fertilisation is also a possibility.

43 Cunningham, vol. III, p.297.

44 Entry in journal for 15 Dec. 1840: 'Went to Constantinople: saw a public auction of the effects of a pasha retired; came back by Galata; got some colours in the lump; took them to a coachmakers to be gound.' op.cit.,vol. III, p.348.

45 Op.cit., vol. III, pp.336.

46 Gustave Flaubert, for example, was shown illuminated manuscripts and miniatures on his visit to Istanbul in 1851.

47 Op.cit., p.325 'In leaving Vienna, we seemed to have left all art and pictures behind us ... We have before us an Eastern and an Asiatic people, – a people who possess neither art nor the feeling for art; and who eschew all idea of picturesque representation ...'.

48 Richard Ettinghausen, *Turkish Miniatures from the 13th to the 18th century*, Milan, 1965, pp.23–4.

49 This subject was also treated by David Roberts and J. F. Lewis.

50 Wilkie wrote of the Turks :'...it is in the condition of the ladies their system appears to the greatest disadvantage... they appear excluded from all intercourse with the world.' Cunningham, Vol.III, p.364. He also refers to 'glaring infringements upon the rights of women', op.cit., p.357. I am grateful to Christopher Ferrard for pointing out that the scribe or Arzuhalji was a writer of petitions who would have performed this service for men and women, literate and illiterate. However, it is unlikely that Wilkie knew this.

51 Ibid., p.365.

52 Ibid., vol.III, pp.259–60. Wilkie wrote to Allan: 'When looking about for new food and fuel, pray think of what I ventured to hint at, of an illustration of the Arabian Nights. This is a walk...quite unoccupied, and to which you bring a fund of local circumstance &c at this period quite unknown.'

53 Ibid.

54 W. M. Thackeray, *Notes of a Journey from Cornhill to Grand Cairo*, in *Works*, vol. V, London, 1900.

55 For a discussion of this point, see John Sweetman, *The Oriental Obesession*, Cambridge, 1988.

56 The RSA acquired a collection of Lewis's watercolour copies of paintings by these artists in 1853.

57 John Ruskin, *Academy Notes*, London, 1904, p.74.

58 The painting, until recently known by this title, clearly represents a departure *from* the island of Venus.

59 Samuel Johnson, *The History of Rasselas, Prince of Abyssinia*, 1759.

60 Kenneth Bendiner, *The Portrayal of the Middle East in British Painting 1835–1860*, PhD Thesis, Ann Arbor, Michigan, USA, 1979, p.14.

61 Loc.cit. Bendiner also points out that Hunt had attempted to join A. H. Layard's expedition to Mesopotamia as a draughtsman in 1853.

62 Thomas Seddon recorded that Hunt disapproved of his wearing eastern dress. However, in Hunt's self-portrait of 1875 he wears Syrian costume.

63 Statement by the artist's brother (*Athenaeum*, 22 March 1879, p.386); quoted in Tate Gallery exhibition catalogue, *The Pre-Raphaelites*, London, 1984, p.151.

64 Ibid.

65 Ibid., p.153.

66 *The Lamp of Beauty: writings on art by John Ruskin*, ed. Joan Evans, Oxford, 1980, pp.76–8.

67 Ibid., p.78.

68 Steegmuller, 1972, p.74.

69 Steegmuller describes Flaubert as 'one of the world's great sensitives', op.cit., p.11. Flaubert made reference to his nervous temperament throughout his life.

70 Steegmuller, 1972, p.135.

71 Ibid. p.222.

72 Ibid., pp.78–9.

73 Letter to his mother, 5 Jan. 1850, ibid., pp.74–5.

74 Ibid., p.81.

75 Ibid., p.112.

76 Loc.cit.

77 Steegmuller, 1972, p.220.

78 Edward Said discusses the essential egoism of most Western perceptions of the East. Of Chateaubriand, for example, he writes: 'What matters about the Orient is what it lets happen to Chateaubriand, what it allows his spirit to do, what it permits him to reveal about himself, his ideas, his expectations. The liberty that so concerns him is no more than his own release from the Orient's hostile wastes.' op.cit., p.173.

79 William Hazlitt, essay on 'Lord Byron' in *The Spirit of the Age*, reprinted in *Byron: The Critical Heritage* (see note 13), pp.272–3.

80 Saint-Beuve wrote, in 1843, that Byron and Sade were the greatest inspiration for his generation. Flaubert had been equally influenced by the writings of Byron and de Sade. Of Byron, he said: 'Il ne croyait à rien, si ce n'est à tous les vices, à un Dieu vivant, existant pour le plaisir de faire le mal'. Quoted in Mario Praz, *The Romantic Agony*, p.180.

81 Ibid. p.322.

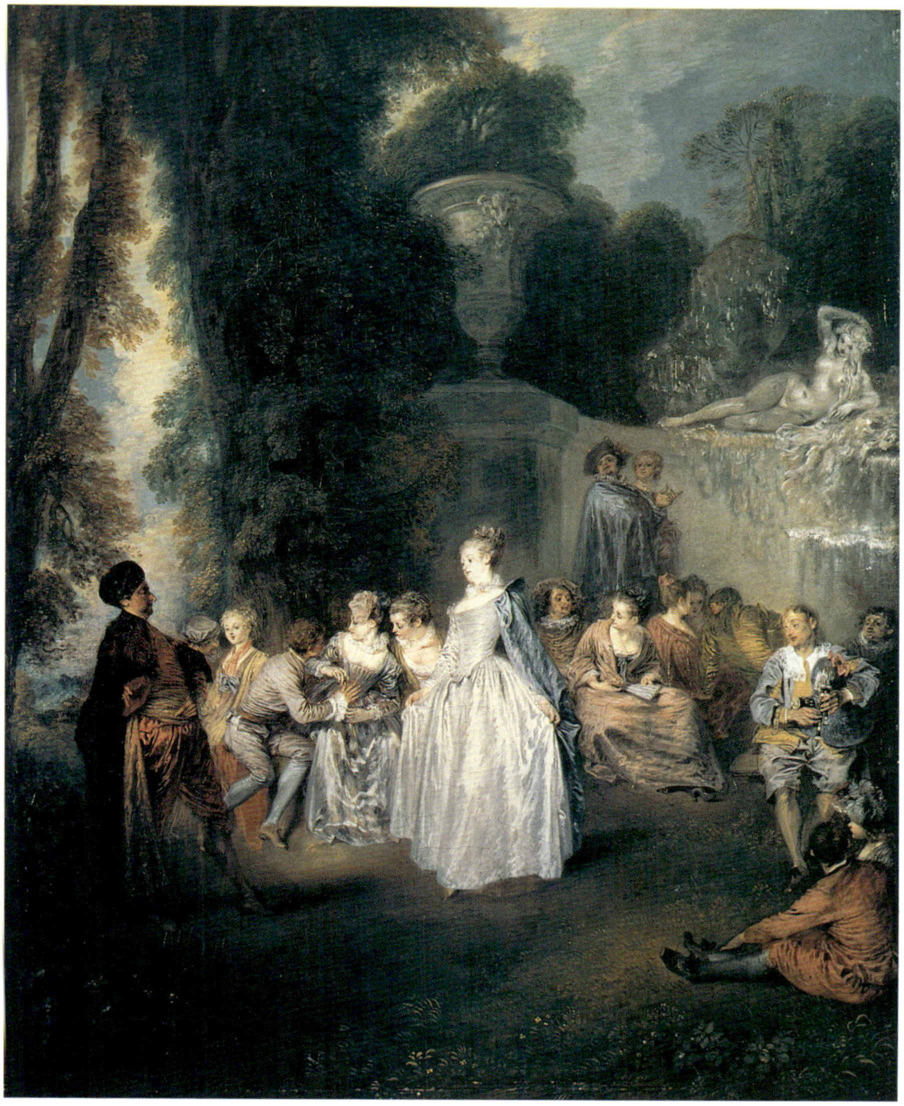

1

JEAN ANTOINE WATTEAU

Fêtes Vénitiennes 1718–19

National Gallery of Scotland, Edinburgh

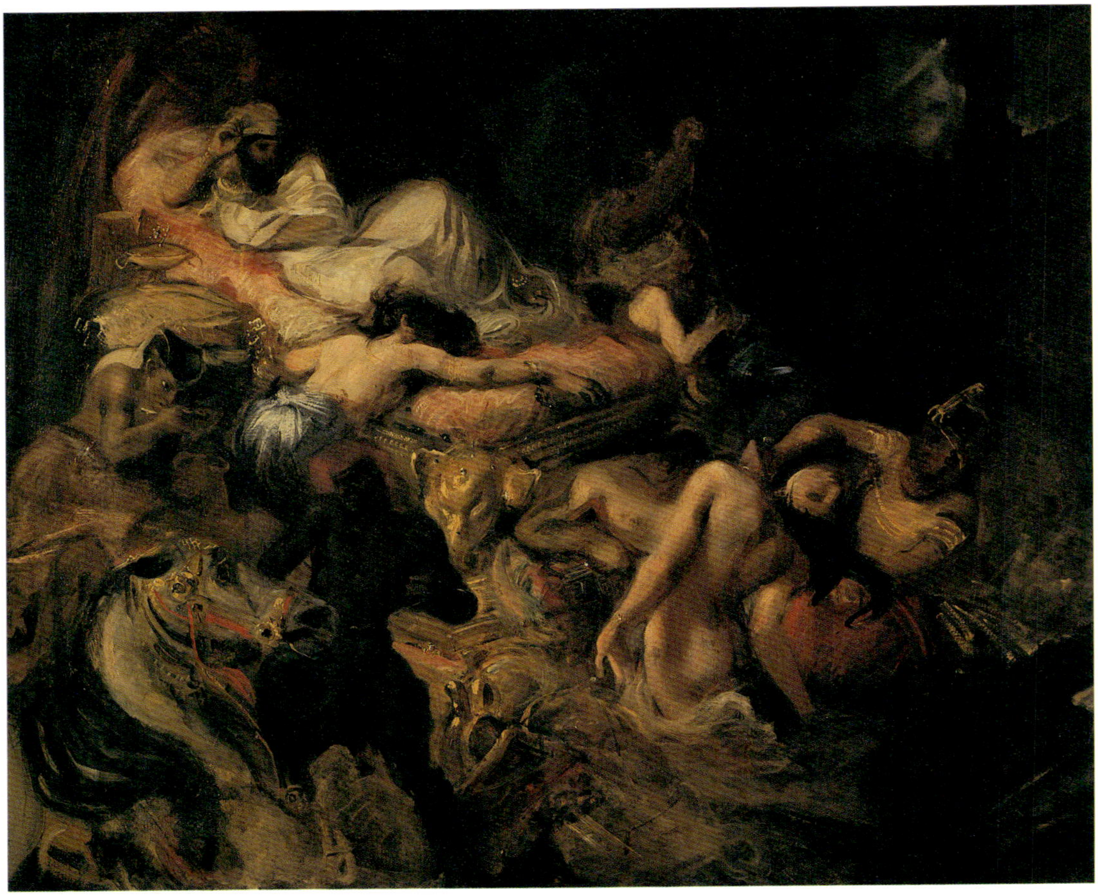

2
EUGENE DELACROIX
Oil Sketch for The Death of Sardanapalus 1826–7
Musée du Louvre, Paris

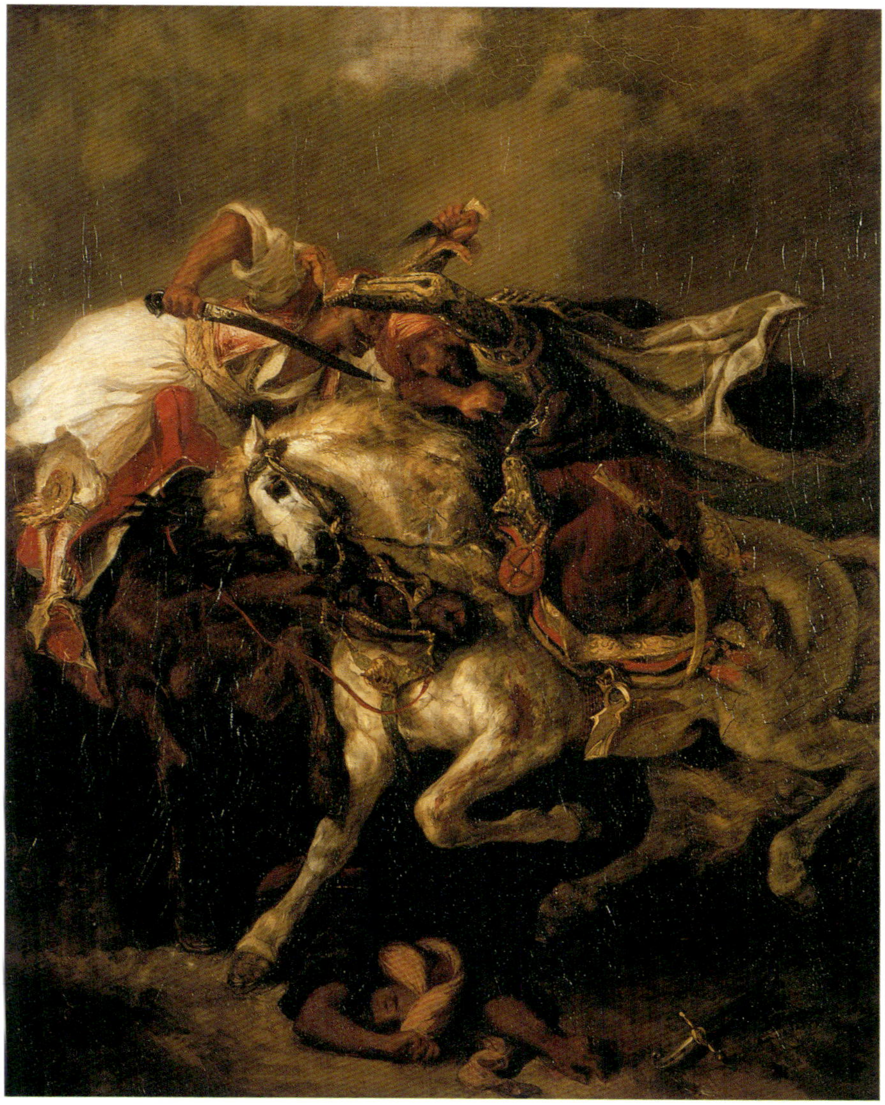

3
EUGENE DELACROIX
Combat between the Giaour and the Pasha 1835
Musée du Petit Palais, Paris

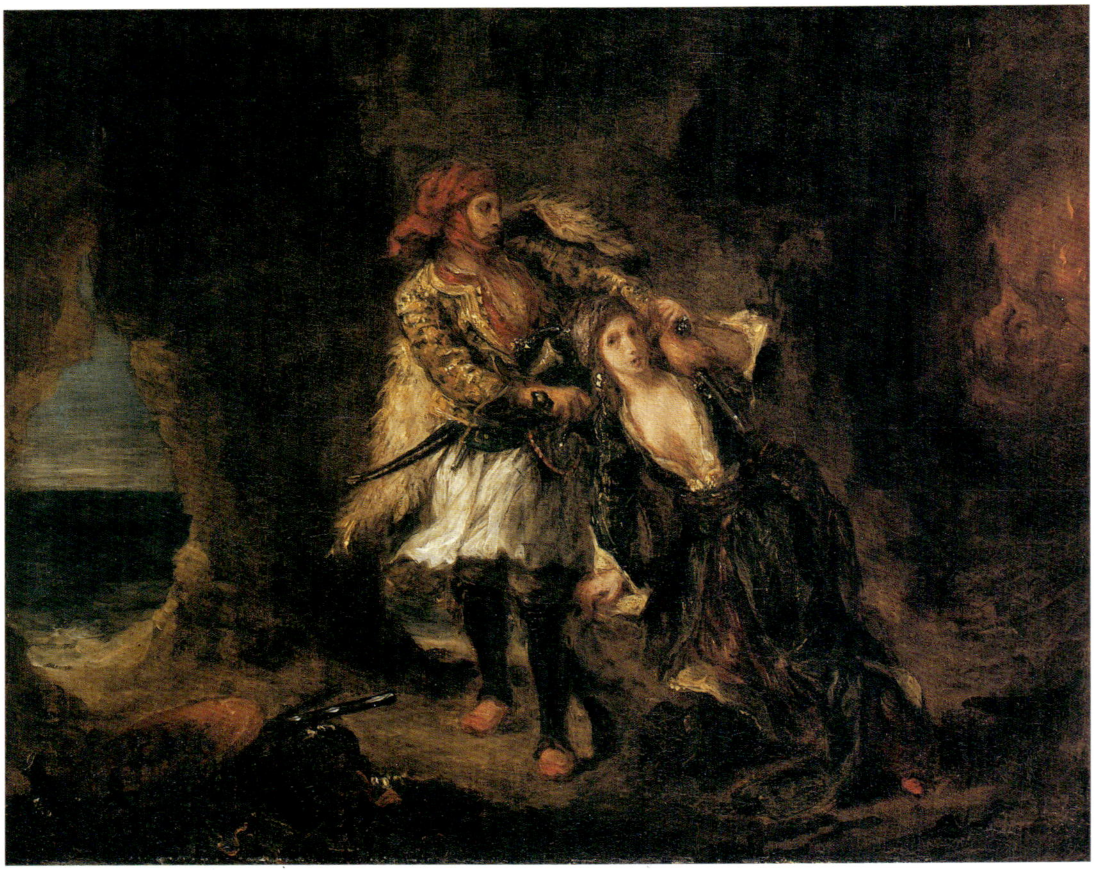

4
EUGENE DELACROIX
The Bride of Abydos c.1849
King's College, Cambridge (Keynes Collection) on loan to the Fitzwilliam Museum, Cambridge

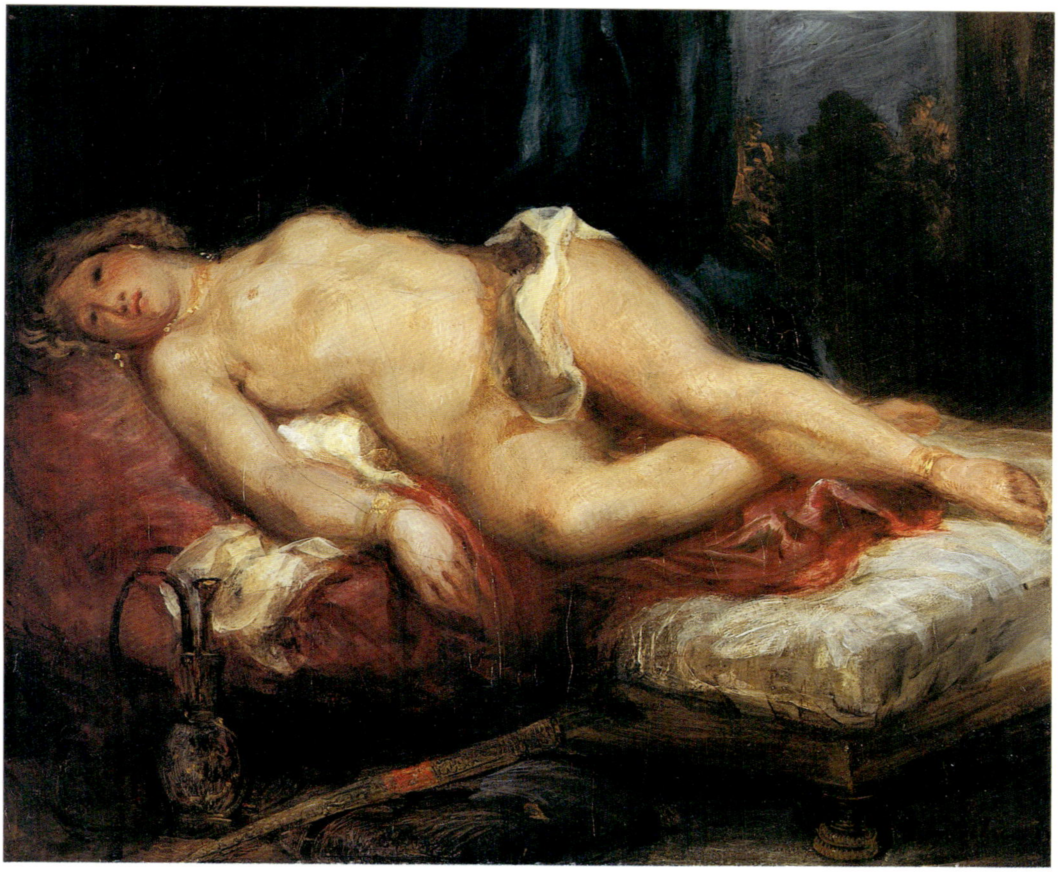

5
EUGENE DELACROIX
Odalisque 1825–8
Fitzwilliam Museum, Cambridge

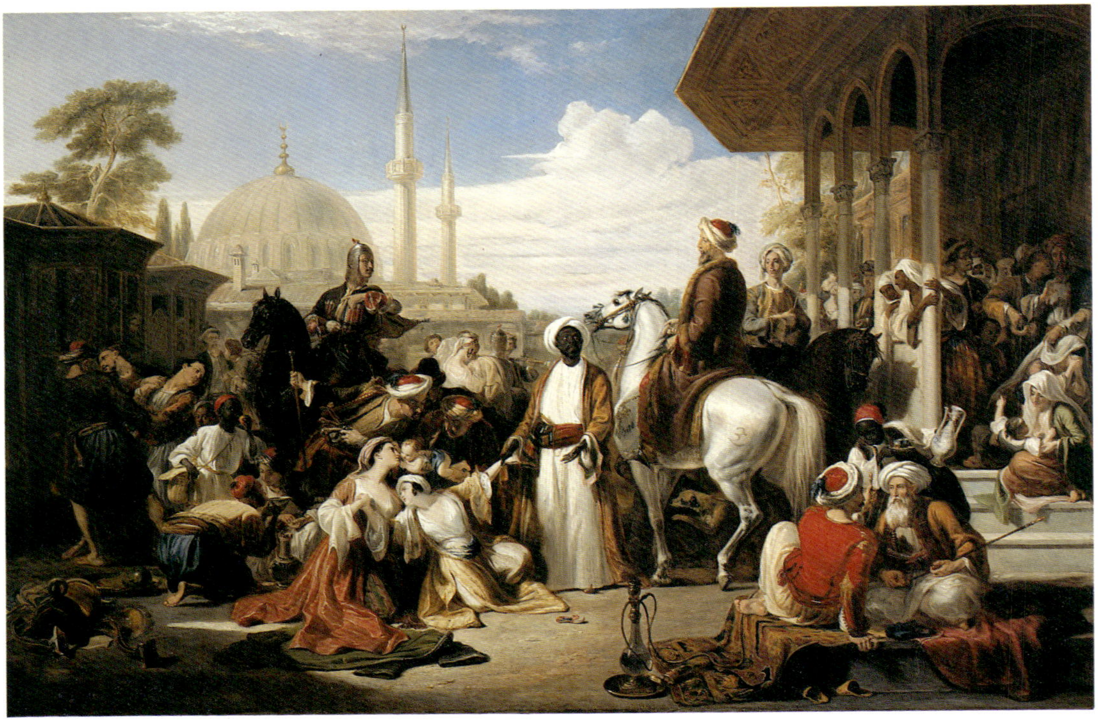

6

SIR WILLIAM ALLAN

The Slave Market, Constantinople 1838

National Gallery of Scotland, Edinburgh

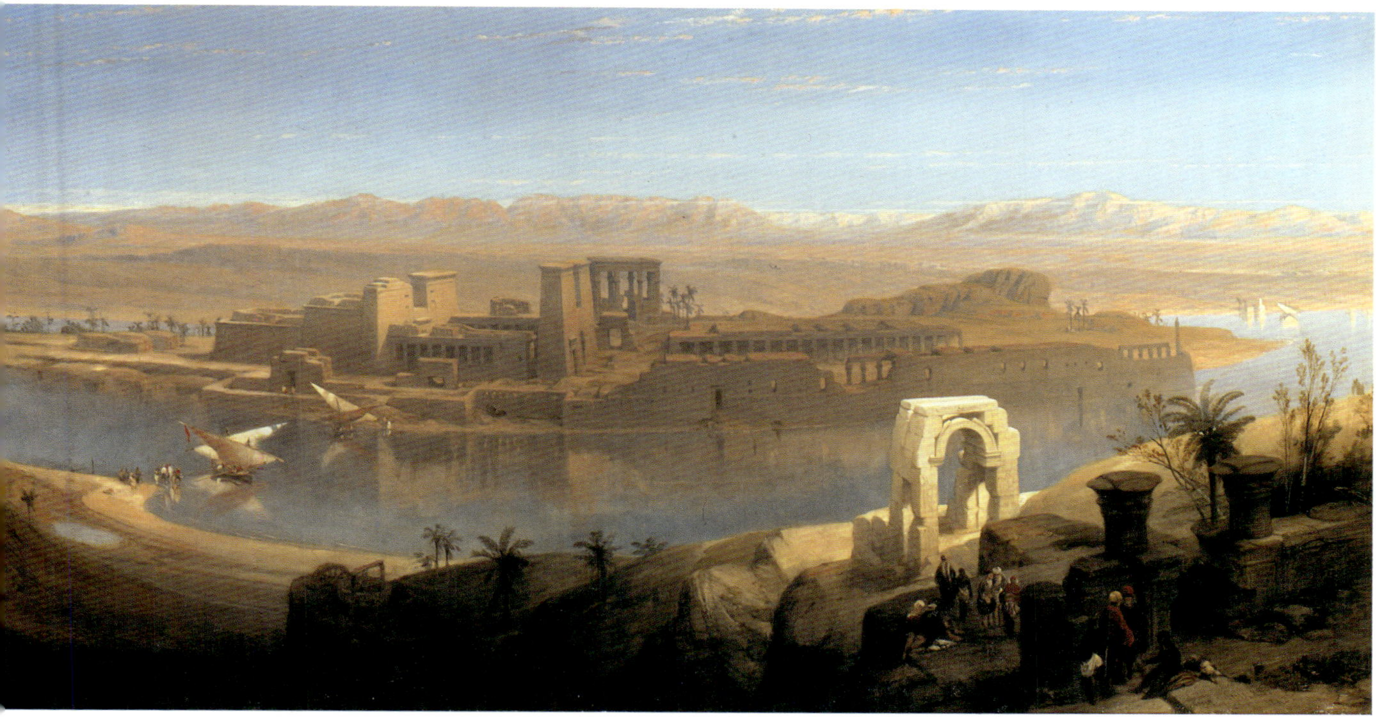

7
DAVID ROBERTS
The Island of Philae, Nubia 1843
Private Collection

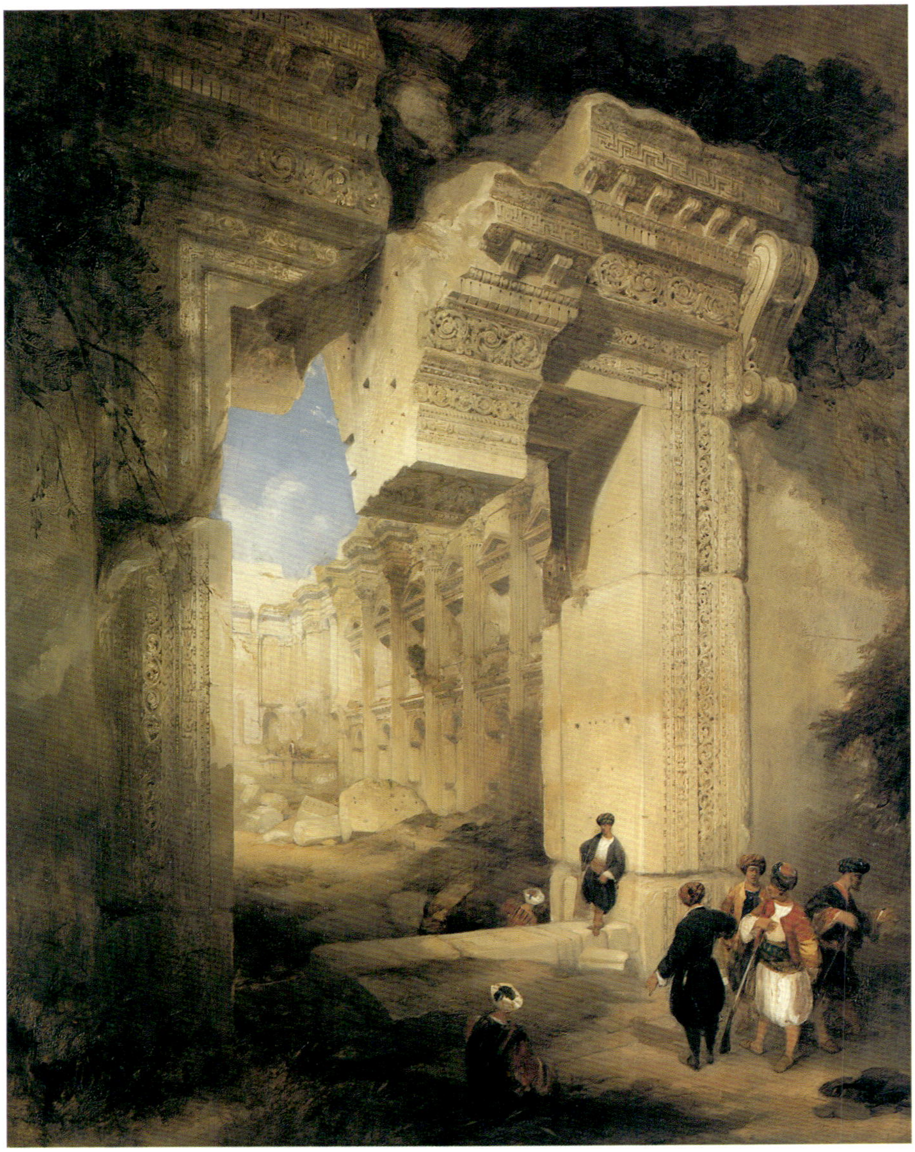

8

DAVID ROBERTS

The Gateway of the Great Temple at Baalbec 1841

Royal Academy of Arts, London

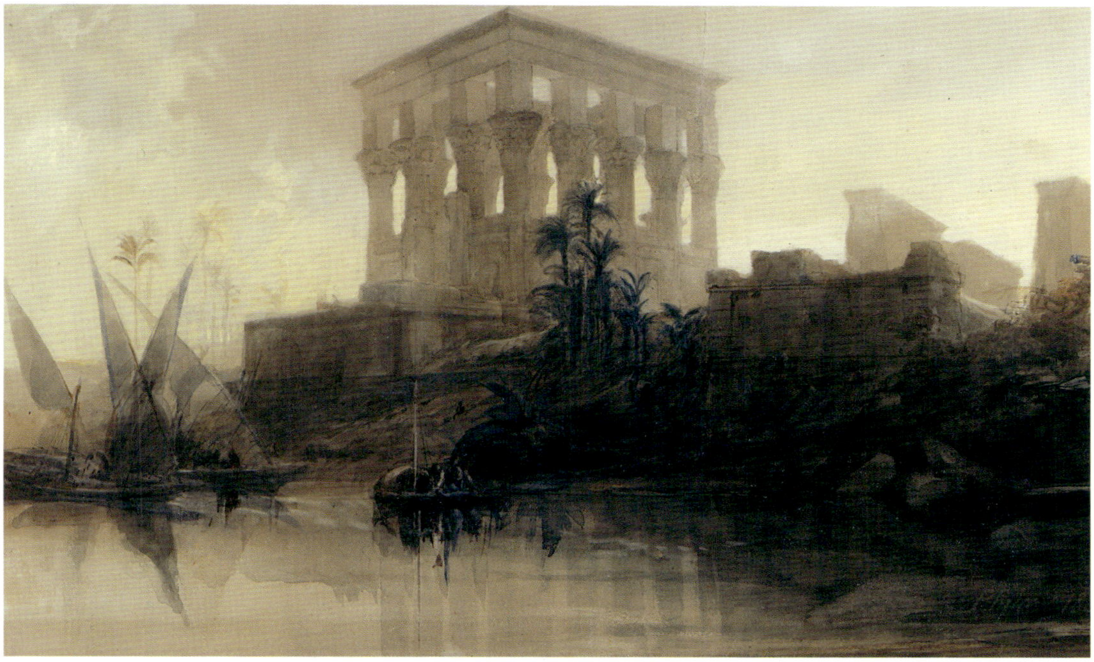

9
DAVID ROBERTS
Temple of Philae 1838
Private Collection

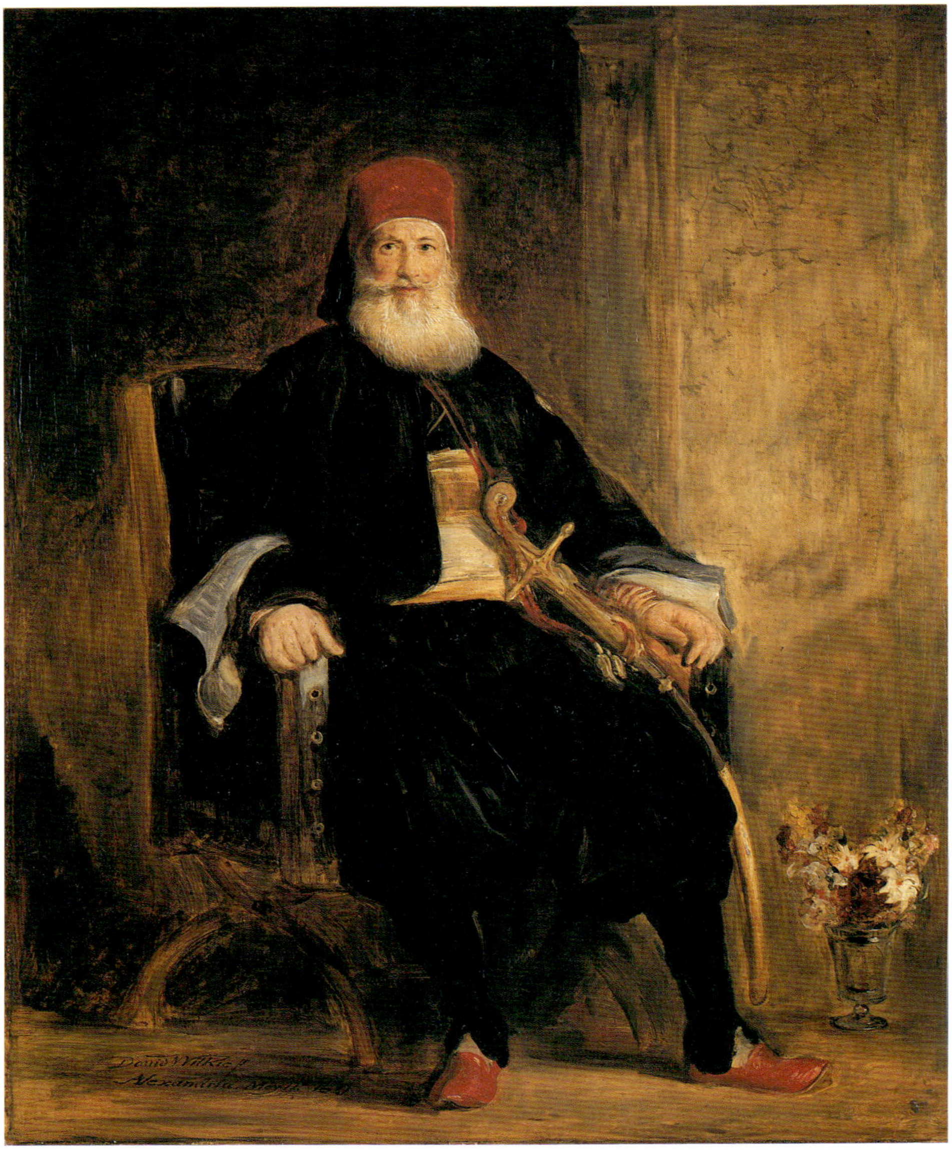

10

SIR DAVID WILKIE

Muhammad Ali 1841

Tate Gallery, London

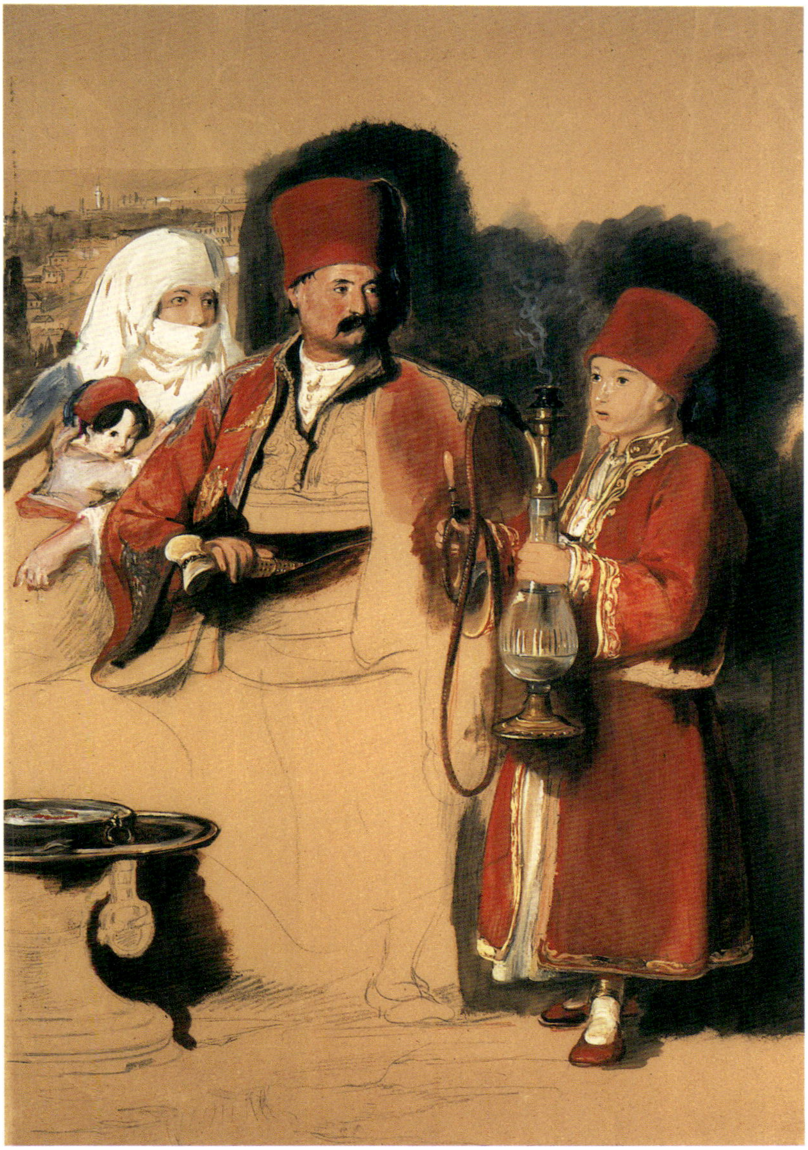

11
SIR DAVID WILKIE
Portrait of Sotiri, Dragoman of Mr Colquhoun 1840
Ashmolean Museum, Oxford

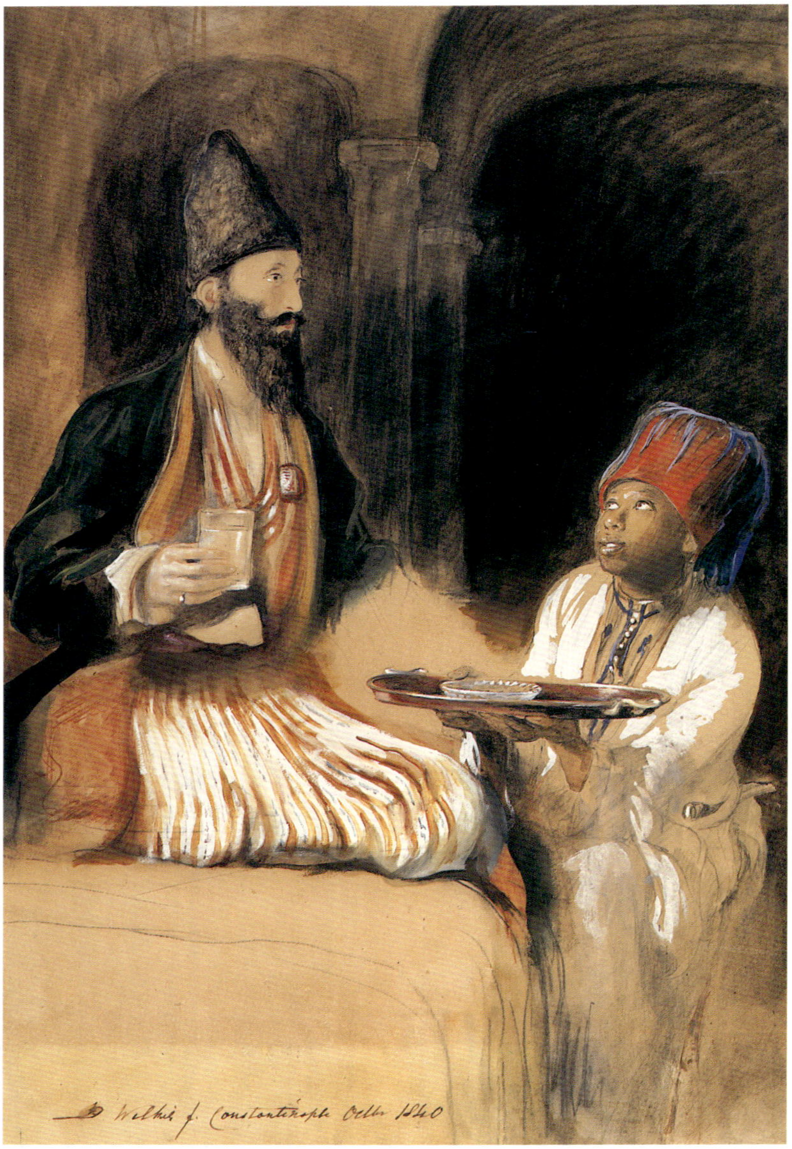

12

SIR DAVID WILKIE

A Persian Prince 1840

Aberdeen Art Gallery and Museum

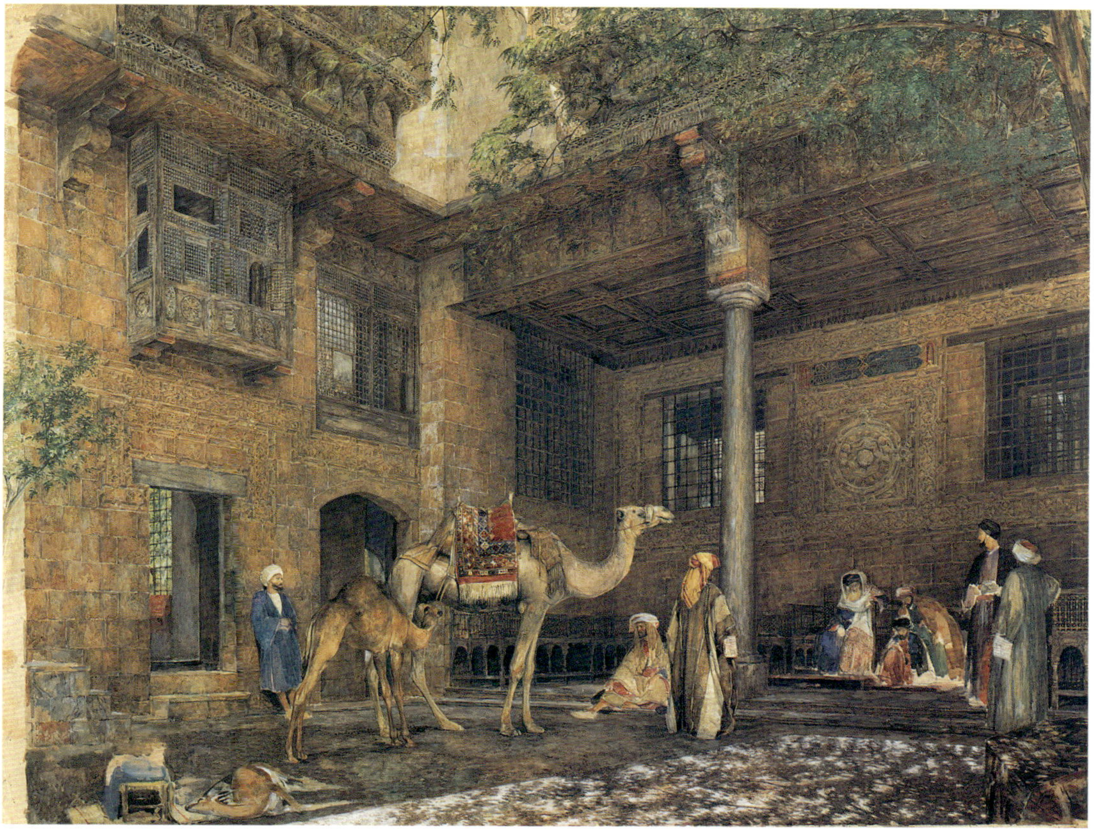

13
JOHN FREDERICK LEWIS
Courtyard of the Painter's House, Cairo c.1851
Birmingham Museums and Art Gallery

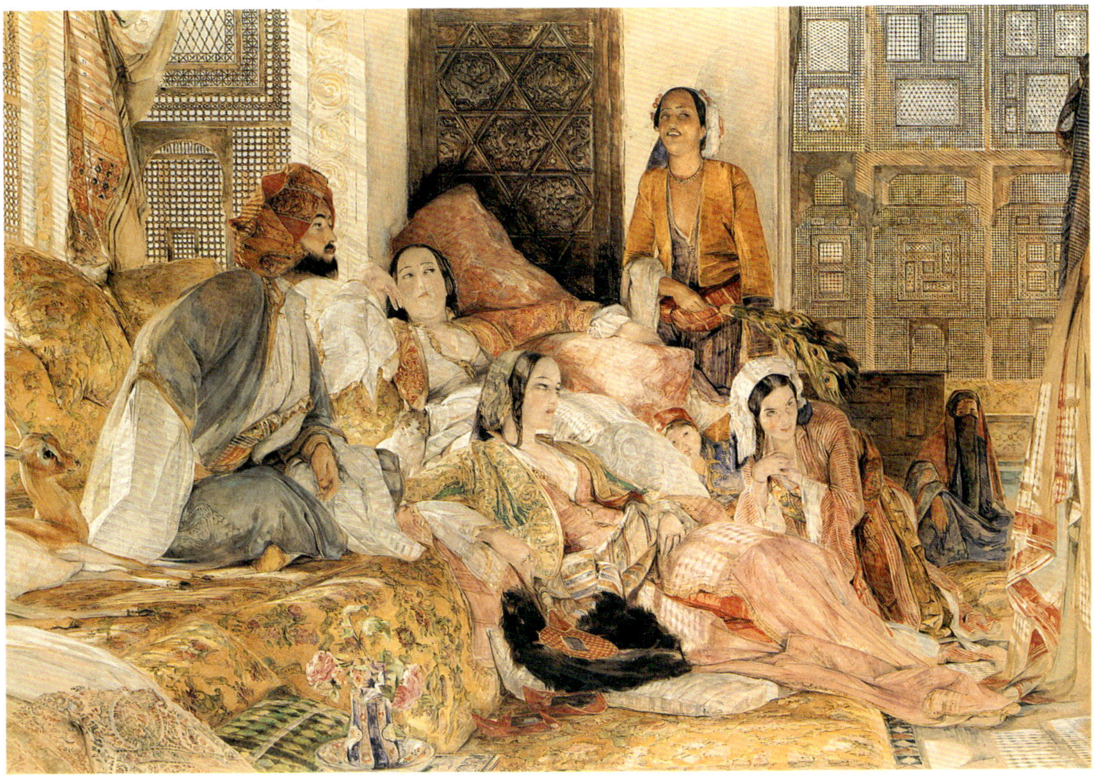

14

JOHN FREDERICK LEWIS

The Harem 1850

Victoria and Albert Museum, London

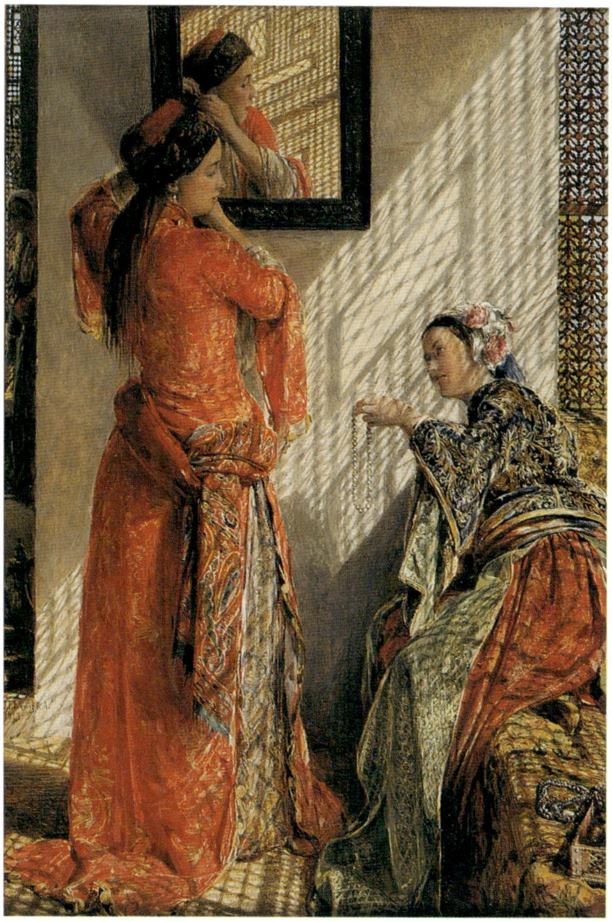

15

JOHN FREDERICK LEWIS

Indoor Gossip, Cairo: a Scene in a Harem 1873

Whitworth Art Gallery, Manchester

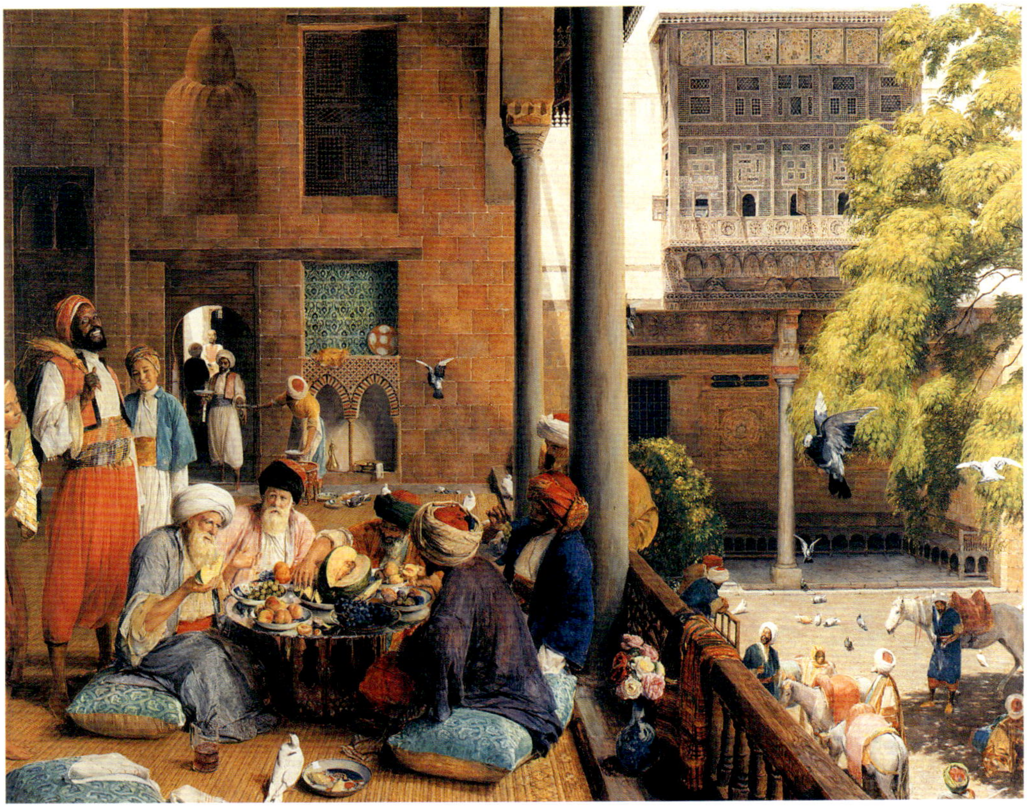

16

JOHN FREDERICK LEWIS

The Mid-Day Meal 1875

Private Collection

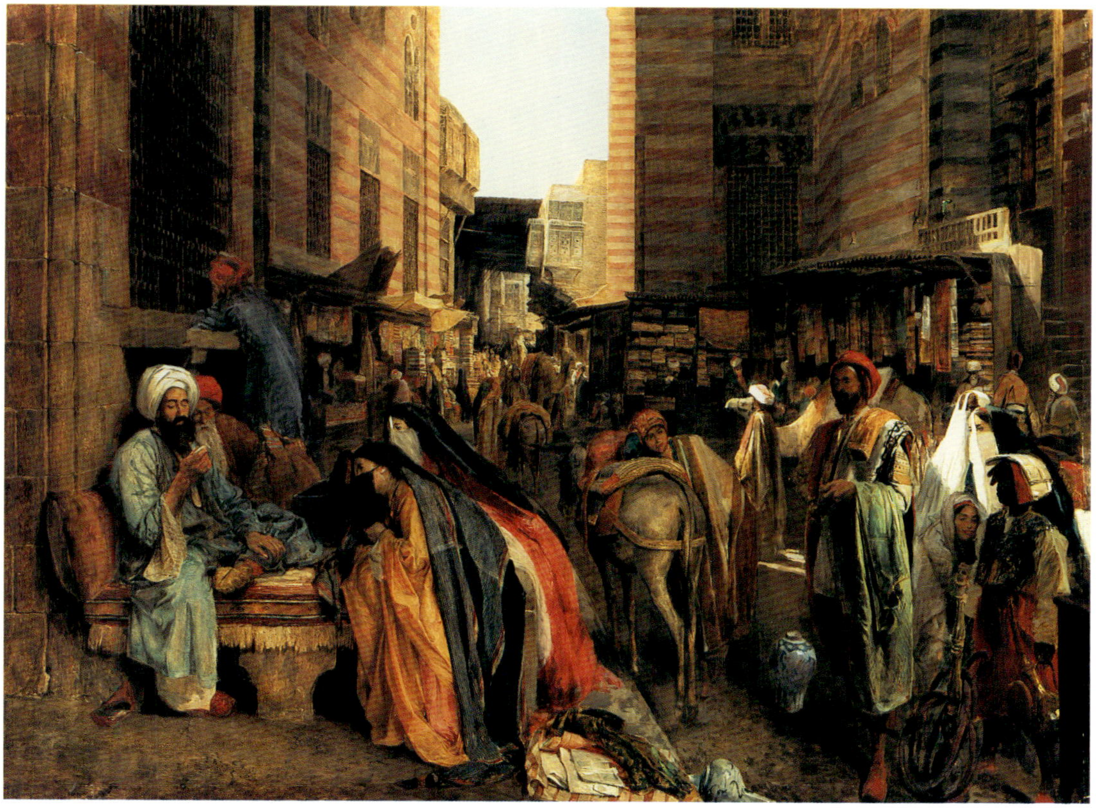

17

JOHN FREDERICK LEWIS

The Street and Mosque of the Ghooreyah, Cairo 1876

Forbes Magazine Collection, New York

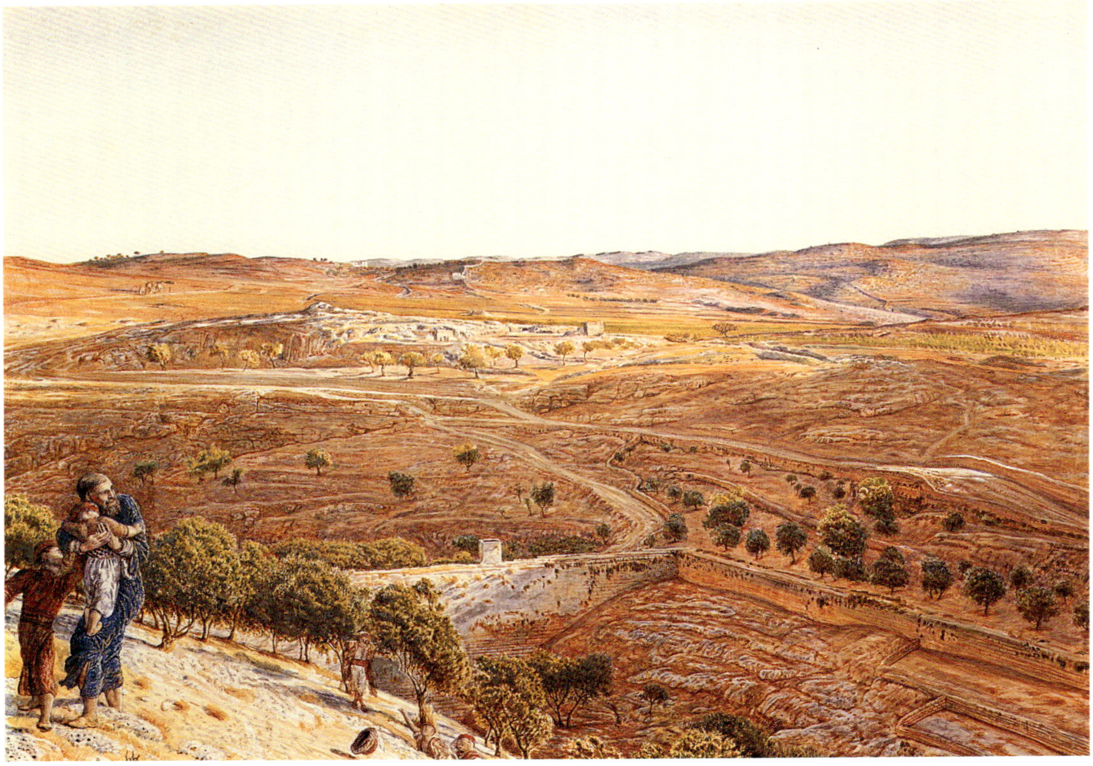

18

WILLIAM HOLMAN HUNT

The Plain of Rephaim from Mount Zion 1855

Whitworth Art Gallery, Manchester

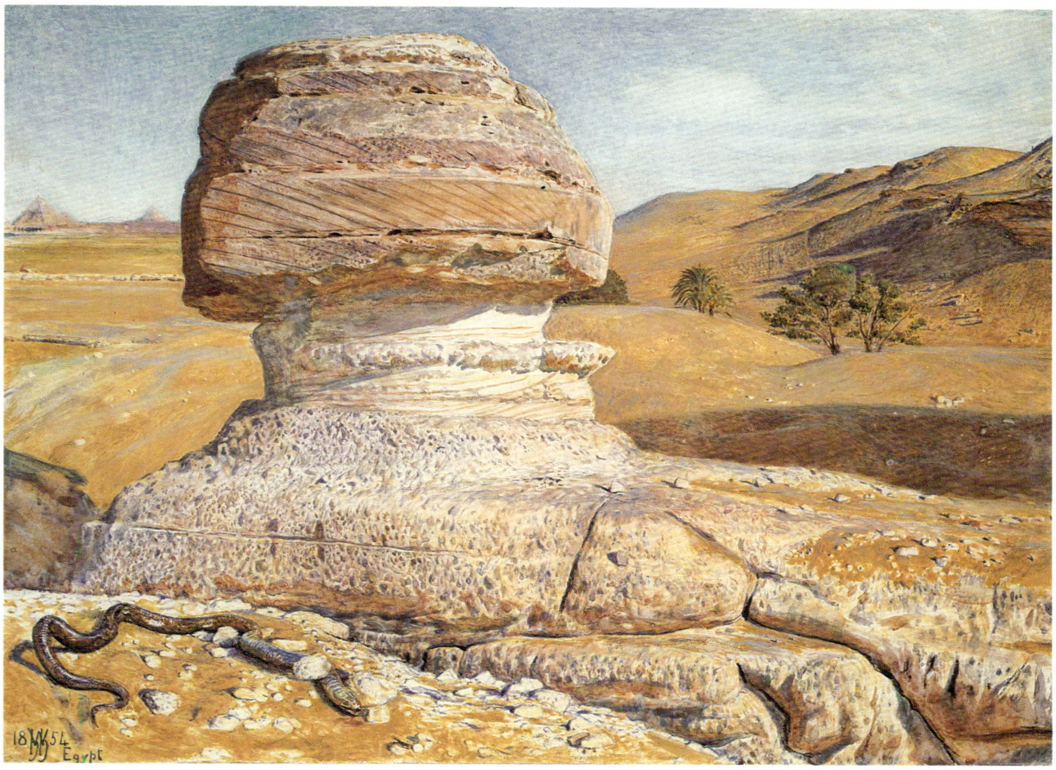

19

WILLIAM HOLMAN HUNT

The Sphinx, Gizeh, Looking Towards the Pyramids of Sakkarah 1854

Harris Museum and Art Gallery, Preston

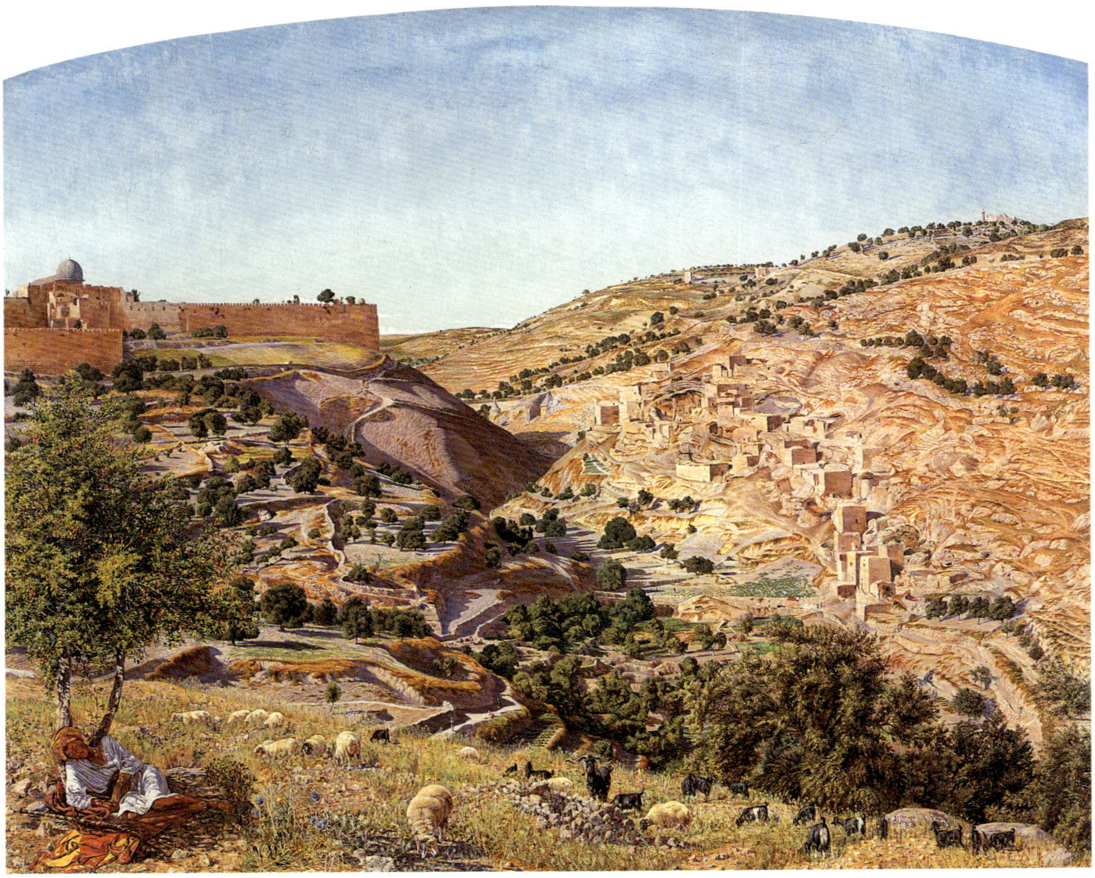

20

THOMAS SEDDON

Jerusalem and the Valley of Jehoshaphat from the Hill of Evil Counsel 1854–5

Tate Gallery, London

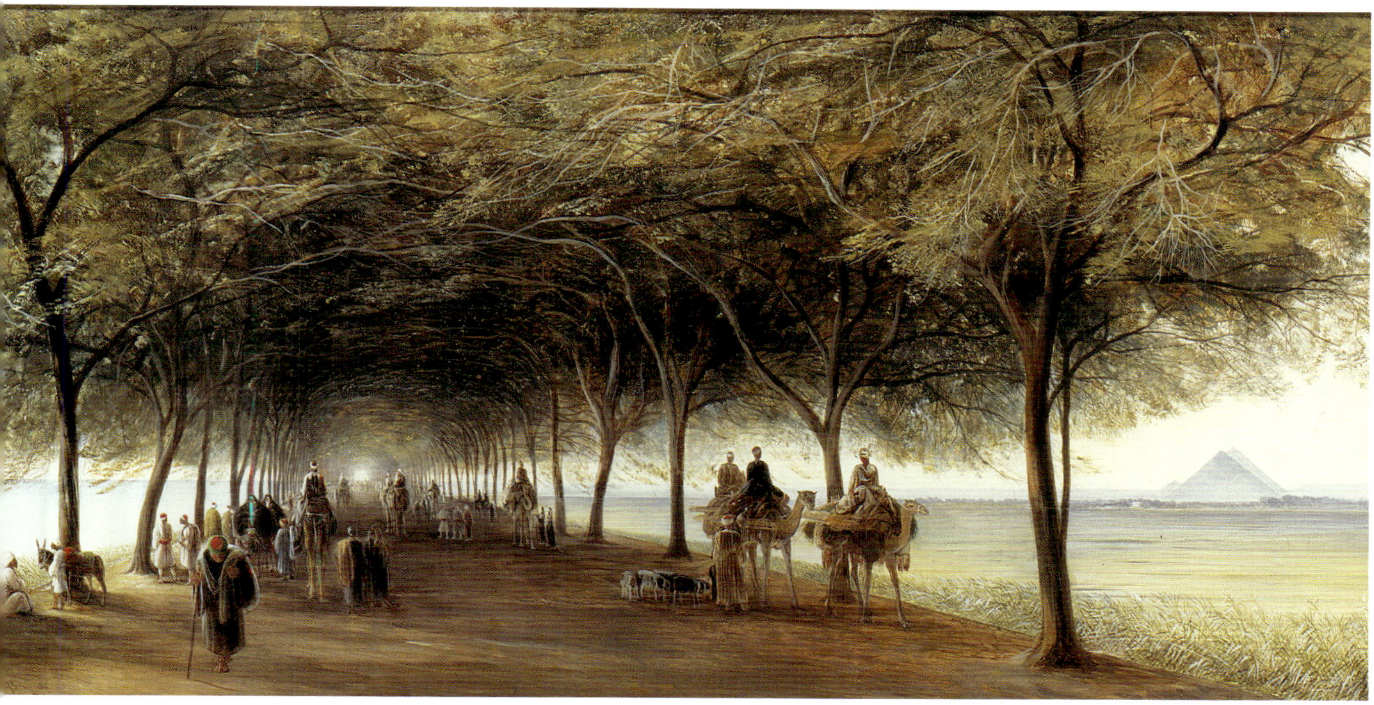

21
EDWARD LEAR
The Pyramids Road, Gizeh 1873
Private Collection

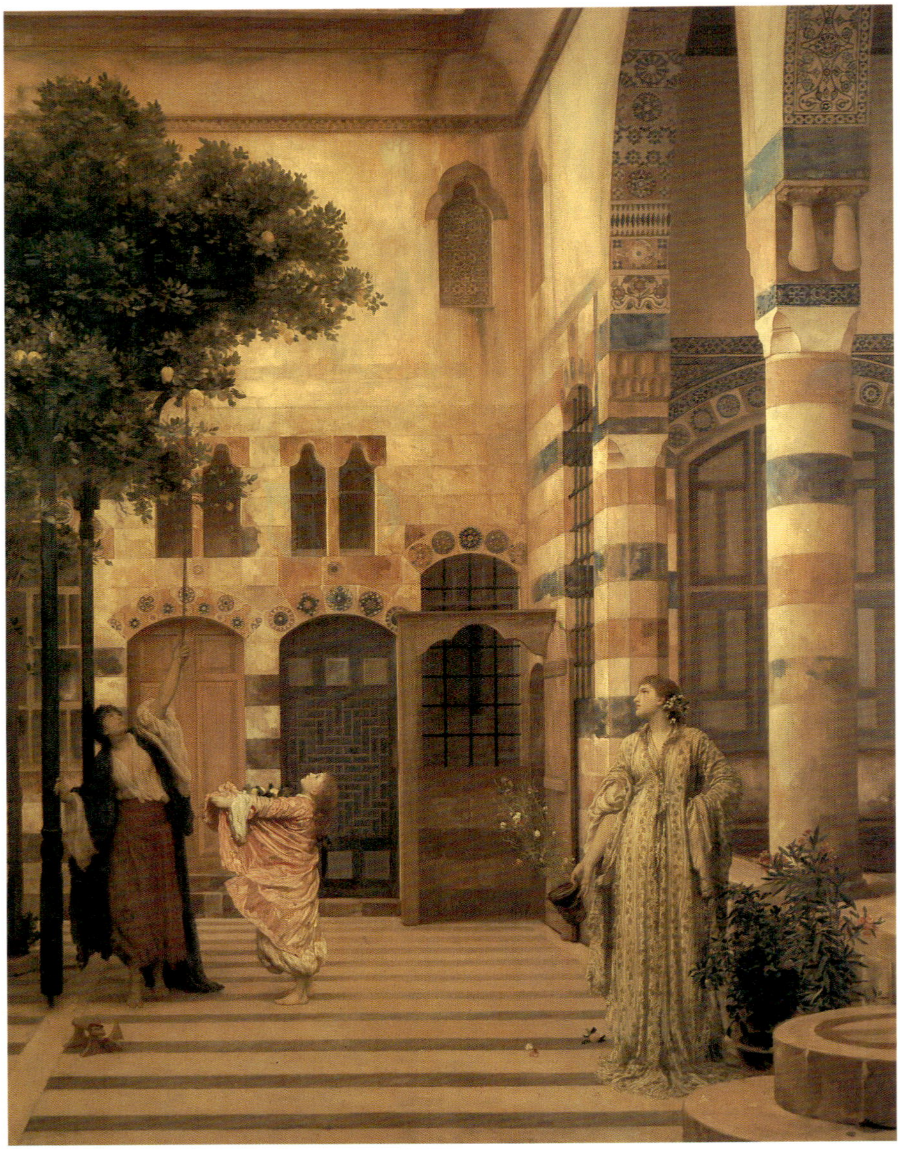

22
FREDERICK, LORD LEIGHTON
Old Damascus 1873–4
Private Collection

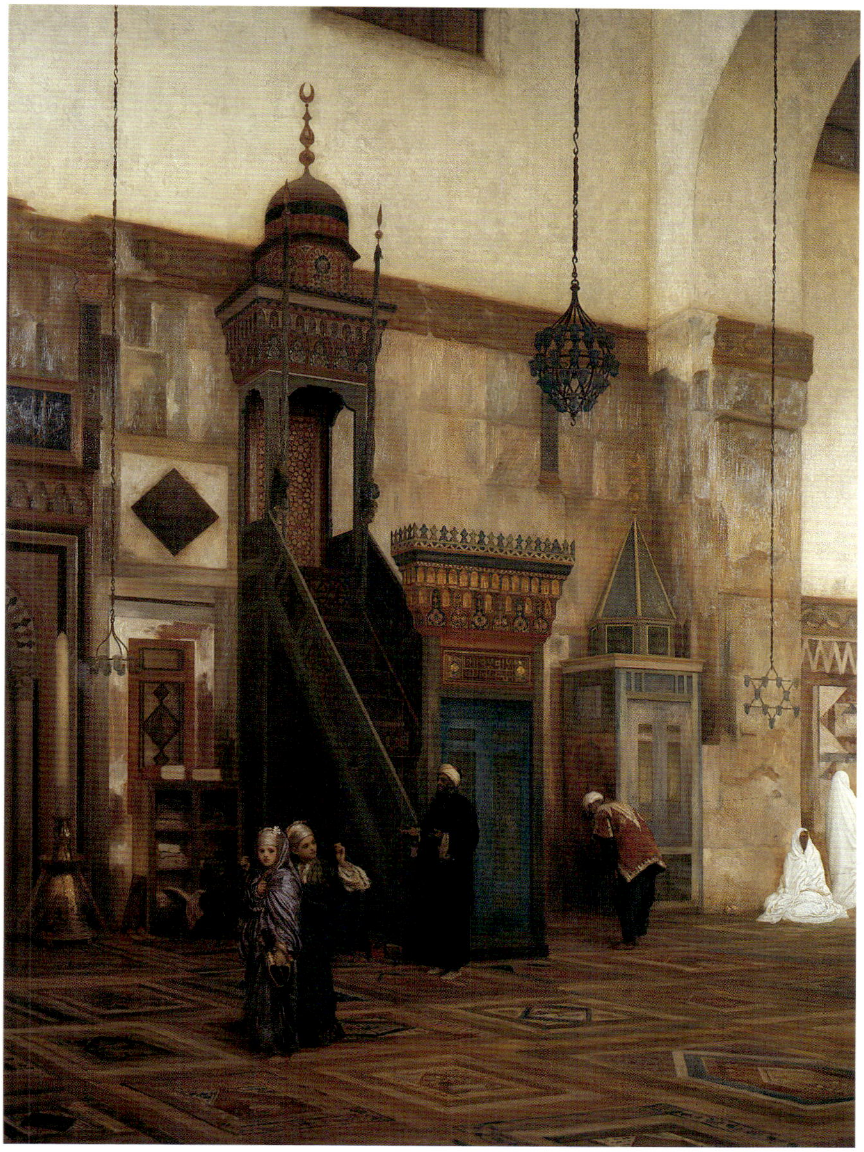

23
FREDERICK, LORD LEIGHTON
Portion of the Interior of the Grand Mosque of Damascus 1873–5
Harris Museum and Art Gallery, Preston

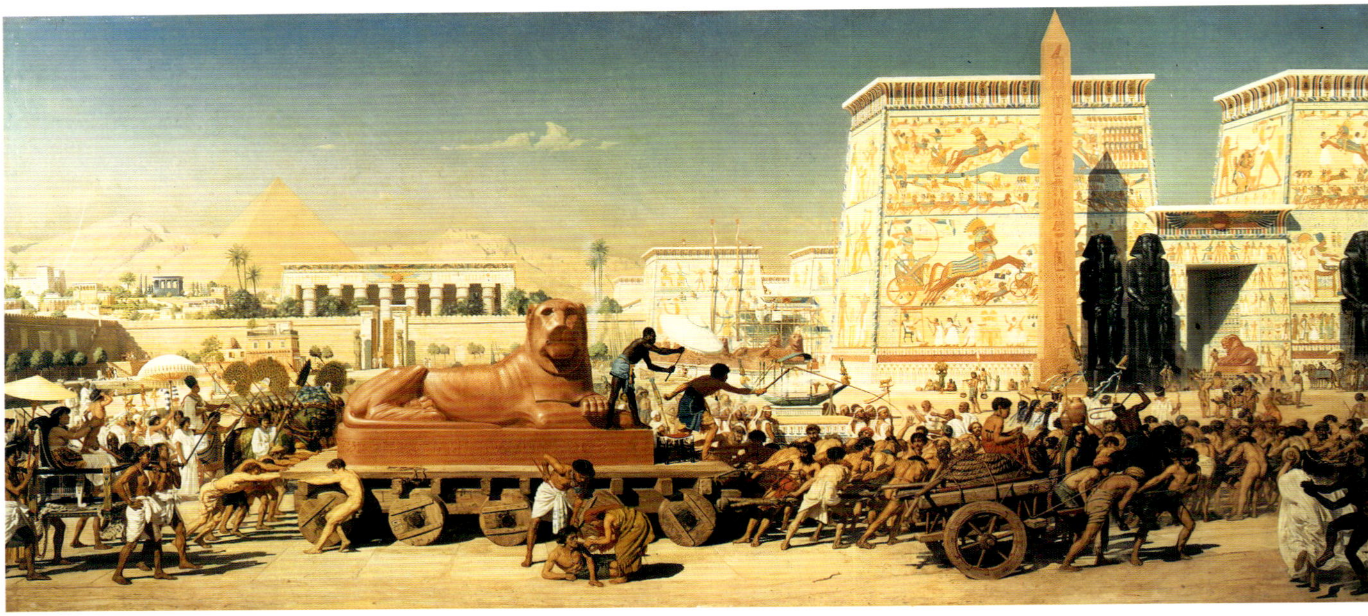

24
SIR EDWARD POYNTER
Israel in Egypt 1867
Guildhall Art Gallery, London

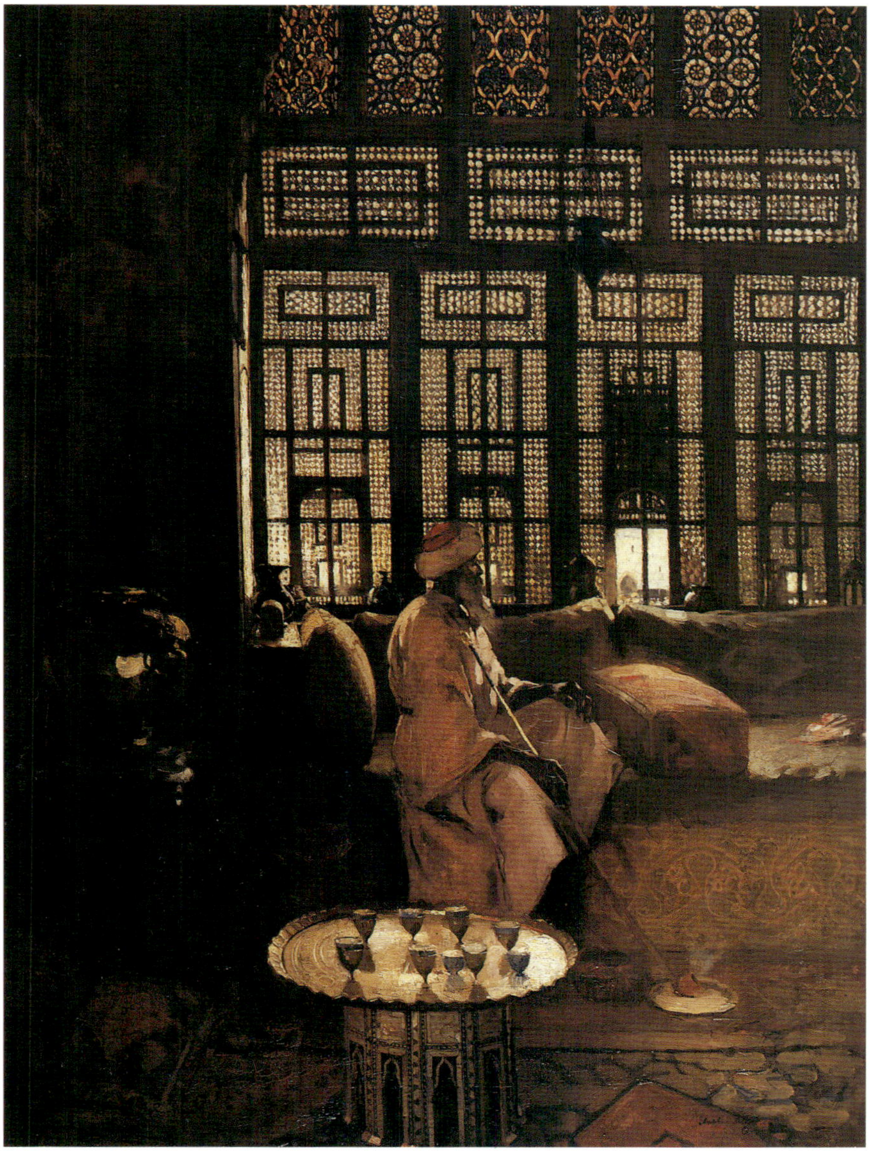

25

ARTHUR MELVILLE

Arab Interior 1881

National Gallery of Scotland, Edinburgh

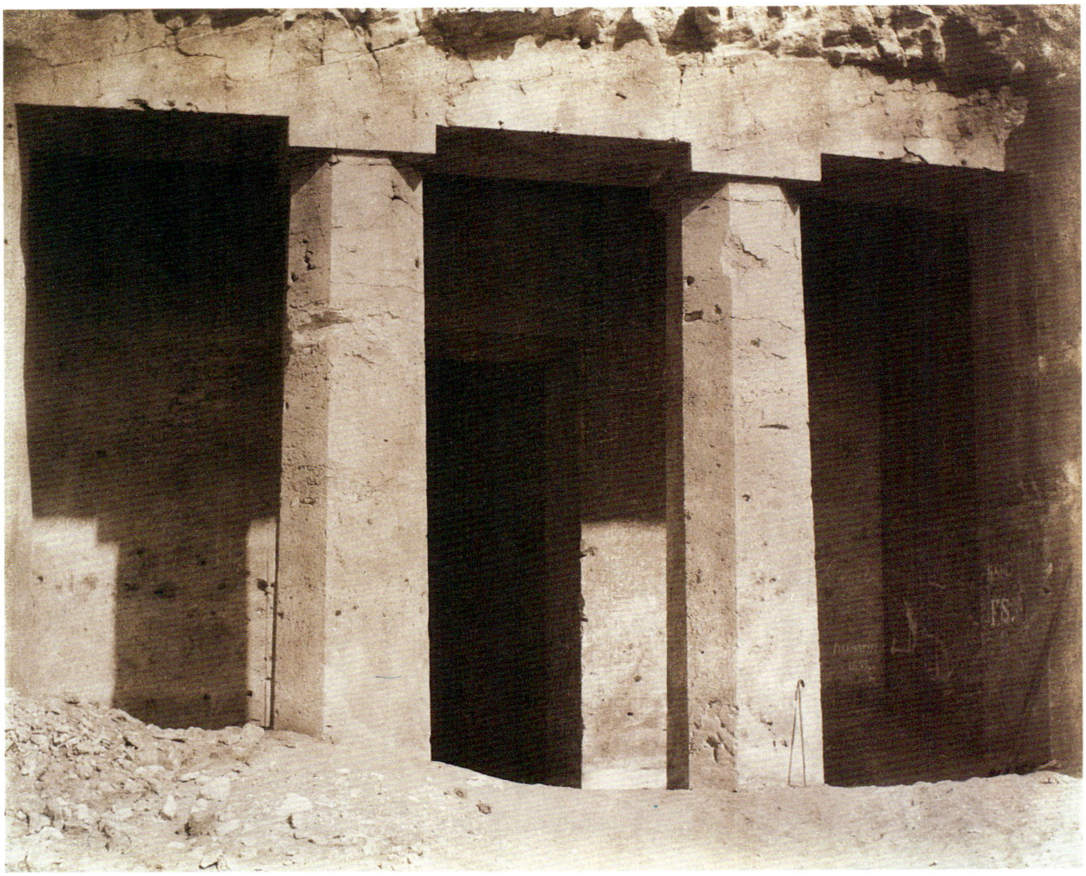

26

FELIX TEYNARD

The Tomb of Amenemhat at Beni Hasan 1851–2

Musée d'Orsay, Paris

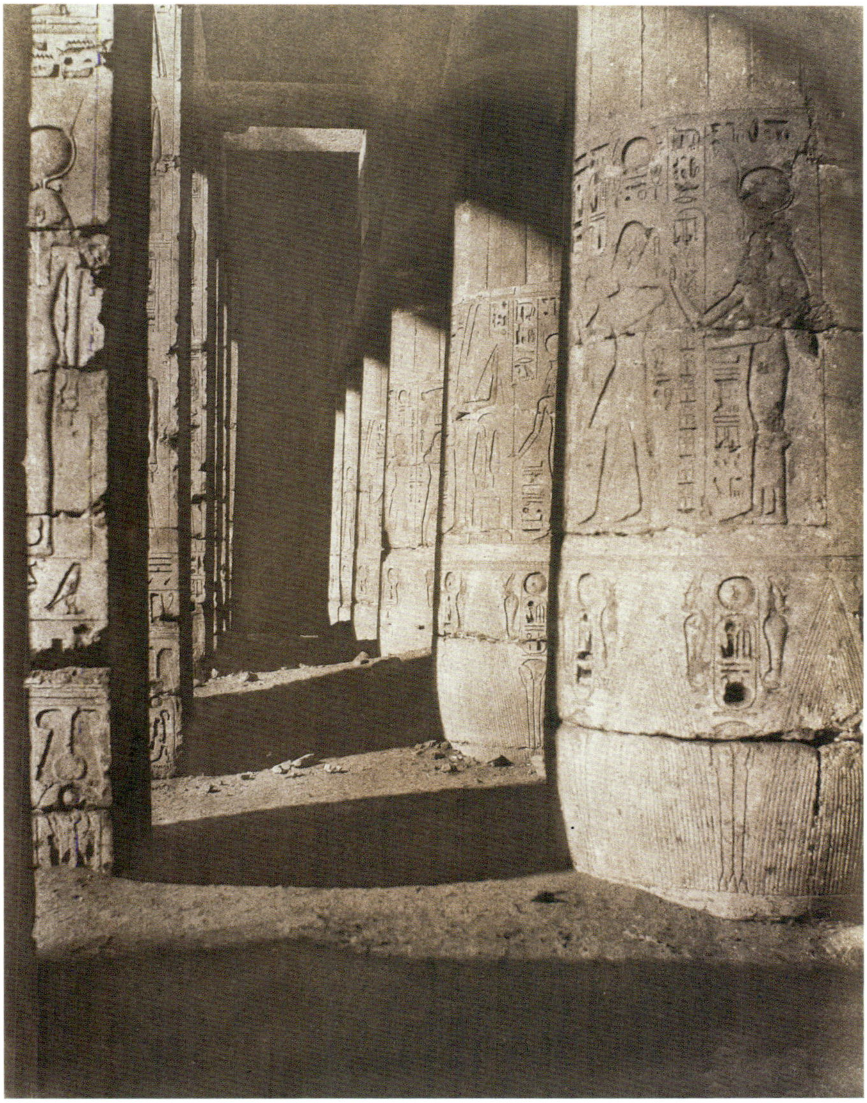

27
FELIX TEYNARD
Medinet Abu, Thebes: Structures at the Back of the 2nd Court of the North-West Gallery 1851–2
Musée d'Orsay, Paris

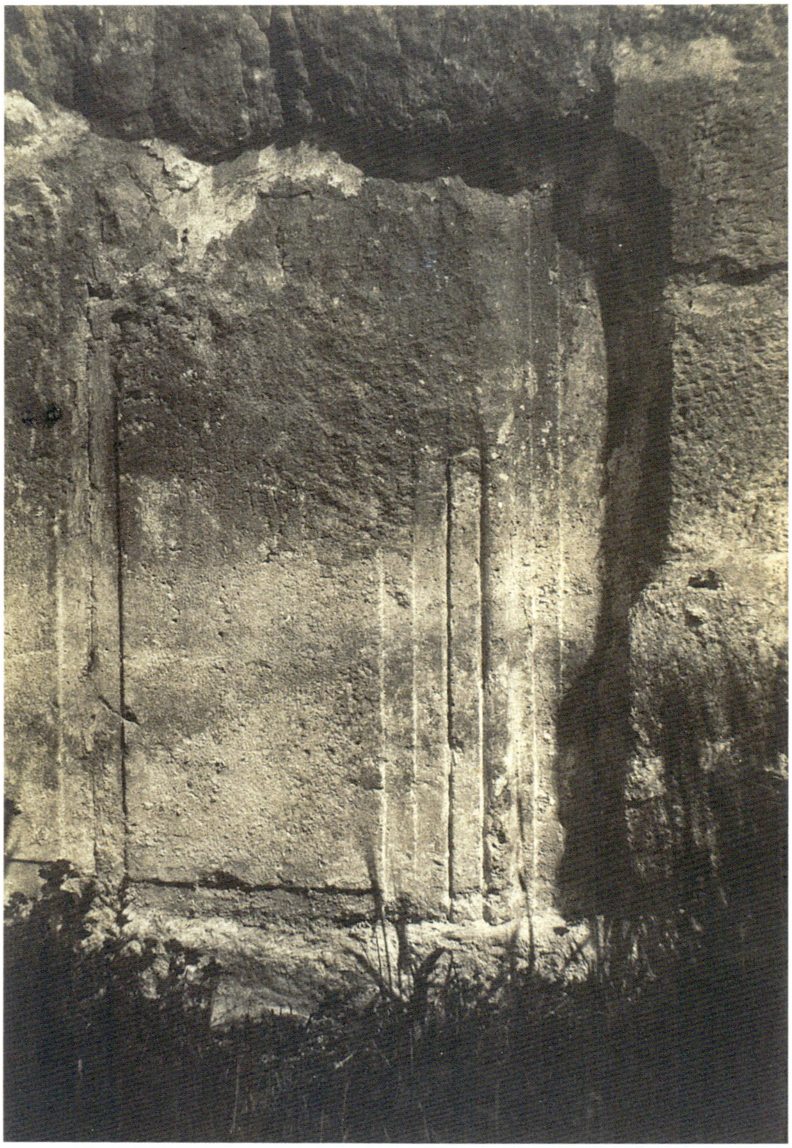

28

AUGUSTE SALZMANN

Jerusalem: The Walls of the Temple, Judaic moulding forming part of one of the Roman Portals 1854

Musée d'Orsay, Paris

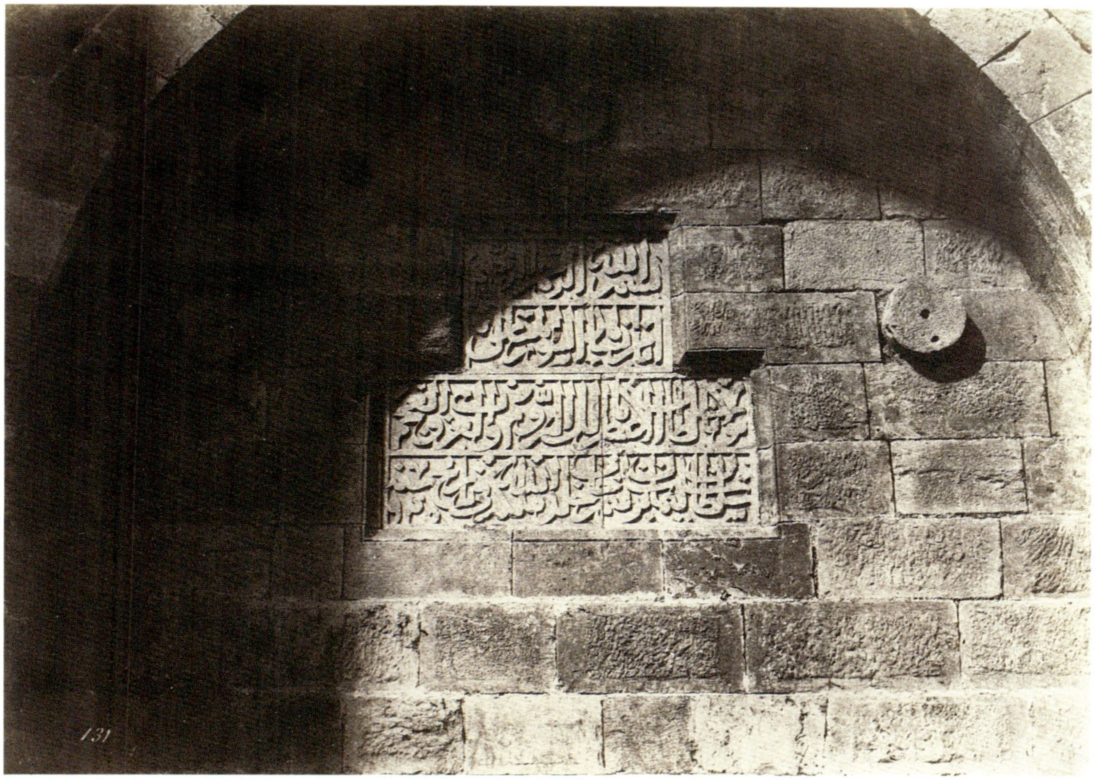

29

AUGUSTE SALZMANN

Jerusalem: The Jaffa Gate 1854

Musée d'Orsay, Paris

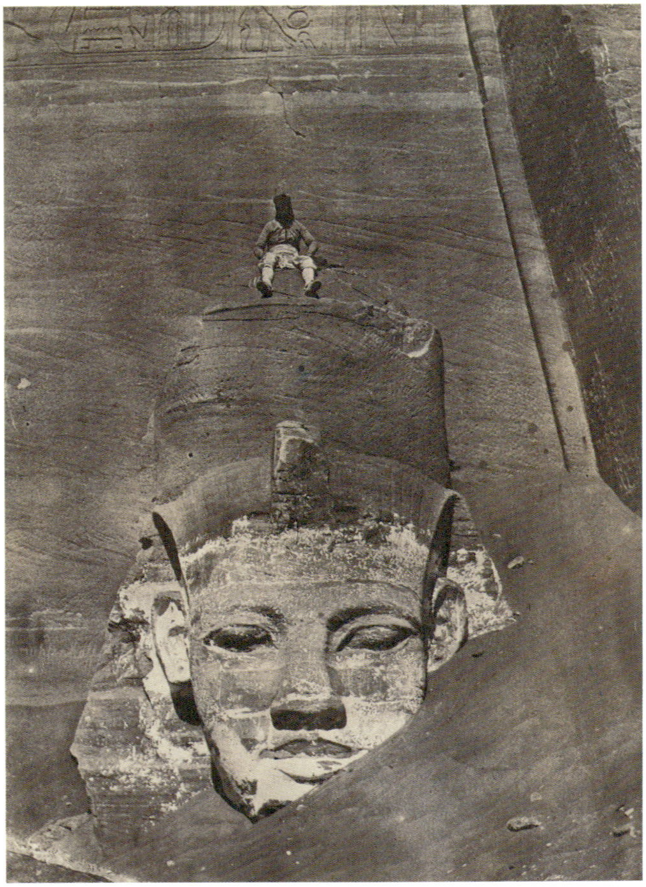

30

MAXIME DU CAMP

Abu Simbel: West Colossus of the Façade 1852

Royal Photographic Society, Bath

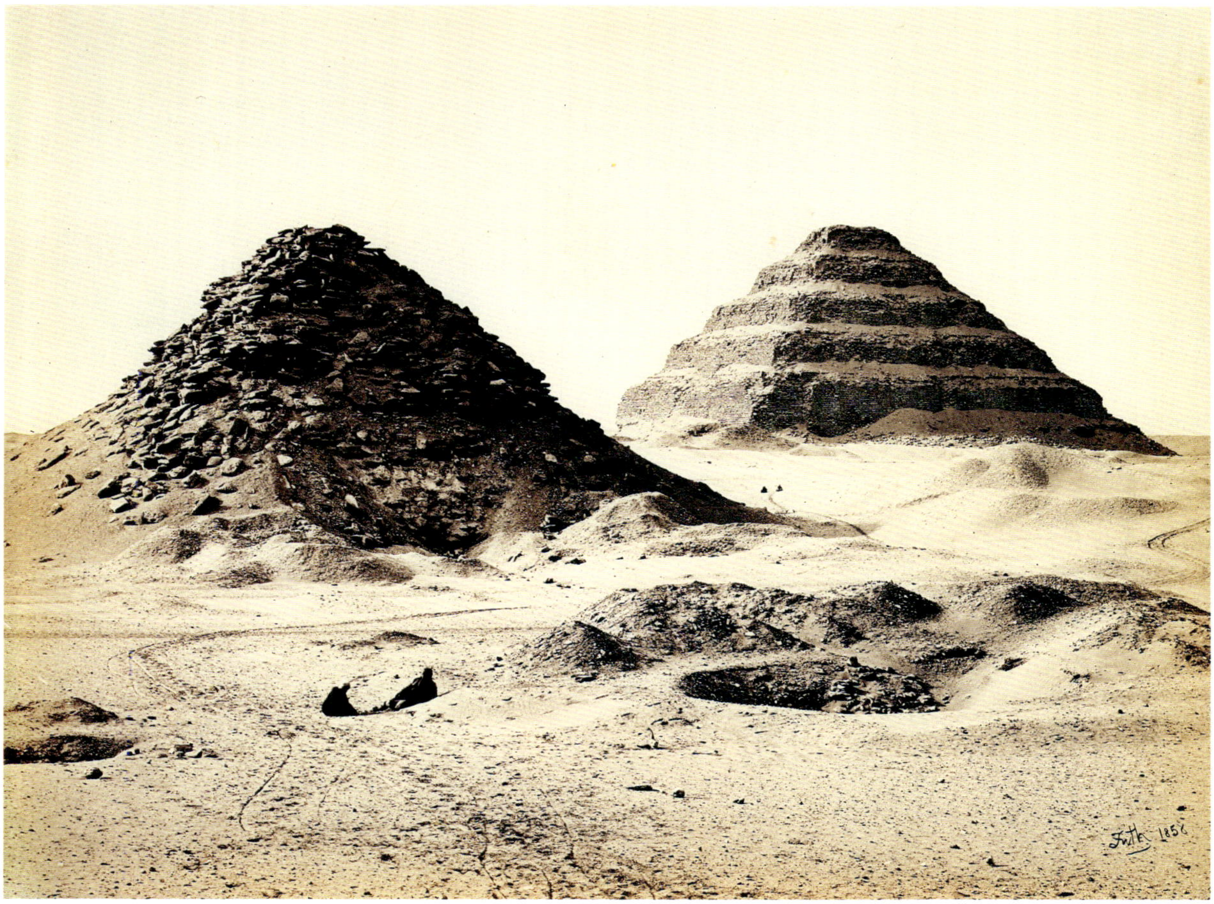

31

FRANCIS FRITH

The Pyramids of Sakkarah from the North-East 1858

Scottish National Portrait Gallery, Edinburgh

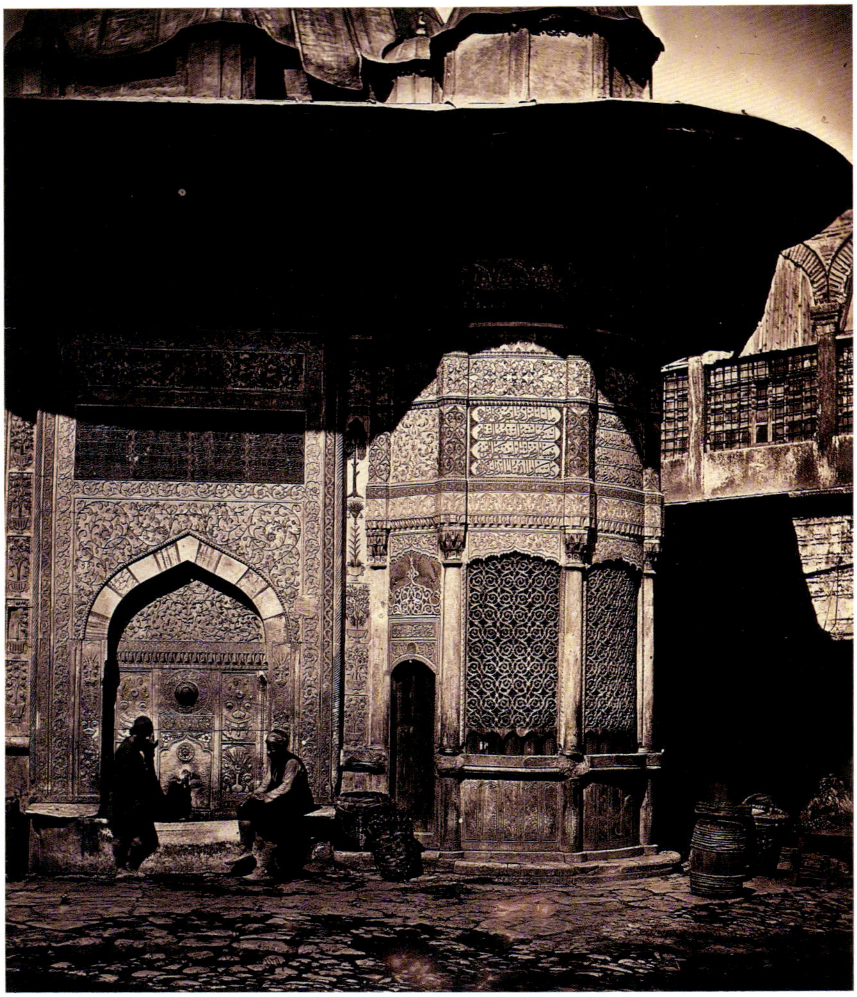

32

JAMES ROBERTSON AND FELICE BEATO

Figures at the Fountain of Sultan Ahmet III, Istanbul 1850s

Scottish National Portrait Gallery, Edinburgh

The Photographer's Vision

Sara Stevenson

IT SHOULD be regarded as one of the great nineteenth-century discoveries that romance and reality are not antitheses: romance is often no more than a tidied or reduced reality, cloaked by decorative flourishes.

One consequence of the Romantic adoption of the Near East was that travellers who came back with carefully written and drawn evidence of the reality – from archaeological to zoological – were met with disbelief. They were victims of a naïve cultural imperialism. The romance was more likely, being closer to common western experience than the astonishing, reality. Imagination falls far behind the reach of the compiler of practical facts.

Curiously, faith and belief stagger under the knowledge that statistics and information are inherently unknowable. It is arguable that the twentieth-century progressive drive has been the urge to master this vast,unknowable mass of information – to bring it down again from the realms of romance into a contained reality, to collect and to codify it.

By an engaging irony, photography was first publicly presented to the world as just such a practical mode of collection, and sold to the French government as efficient, cheap and quick. In 1839, François Arago delivered a speech to the Chamber of Deputies, which was described by Elizabeth Eastlake as:

a masterpiece of scientific summary and philosophic conclusion. He pointed out the immense advantages which might have been derived, 'for example, during the expedition to Egypt, by a means of reproduction so exact and rapid'. He observed that 'to copy the millions and millions of hieroglyphics which entirely cover the great monuments at Thebes, Memphis and Carnac, &c., would require scores of years and legions of artists; whereas with the daguerreotype a single man would suffice to bring this vast labour to a happy conclusion.[1]

The camera's role as a truth-teller is an ambivalent one, but it has had a reputation as an independent, objective machine which made the extraordinary respectable. This strange mediating role put the photographers in an enviable position: they would be believed. The romance of their reality would have the force of accepted truth. In the words of the French photographer, Auguste Salzmann, photographs were 'brutally conclusive' evidence.[2]

Salzmann's photographs were taken in Jerusalem to demonstrate the truth of Félicien Caignart de Saulcy's dating of archaeological fragments back to the time of Solomon – subject of acrimonious dispute despite his meticulous notations and drawings.

The idea that a photograph was an unmediated truth had particular force in the Holy Land. It appears in Sophia Poole's text for Francis Frith's photograph, *Jerusalem, from the Mount of Olives*:

Nowhere in this series do we so fully recognise the peculiar excellence of photography as in the view before us. In it we have the very reflection of Jerusalem. Artists have represented the Holy City; but while we have admired their works, we have lamented an inevitable want of perfect exactness. The first feeling in looking at them with those who had seen what they purport to portray has been disappointment; with those who had not, distrust. Here, the first feeling is the satisfaction produced by confidence; and as with a much-loved face, such a truthful record is of more value than an elaborately beautiful picture.[3]

In this argument, the idea of the specific takes over from the ideal; the artist as mediator is dismissed as a troubling interference.

The concept of photographic art is positively antipathetic in such a context. Here the photograph is seen as a mirrored truth, an object fit for contemplation more akin to a relic than a devotional painting. This sense of physical reality also appears in the idea that the viewer is transported to the place and, by wielding a magnifying glass, can climb into a photograph, move closer to its distance and detail. The panoramic photographs of James Robertson and Roger Fenton serve the same purpose, surrounding the viewer in a two-dimensional image that turns into three dimensions through his own circling and focusing eye.

In certain areas of photography, practitioners inherited clear visual guidelines or definitions – a graphic tradition based on western educational assumptions and taste. Early photographers in Rome or Athens tripped, so to speak, over the easel, fitting their camera tripods into the easel marks, presented with a structure and locations which fed their response. Certain monuments required to be photographed; certain standpoints were formally established. Whether accepting or challenging, the photographers were usually working within a recognisable cultural framework.

There was no dominant or seductive visual tradition – such as the Roman engravings of Piranesi – even for the comparative familiarity of Istanbul, a city linked by its Byzantine history to the western world. The pedestrian art of book illustrators can have been no preparation or effective basis for the great photographers working here. The canvas was largely blank. The Ottoman Empire was enormous, culturally rare, sophisticated and complex. Any western artist's response was likely to lie between shock and astonishment.

Part of this effect is that there was too much in the way of art, architecture and culture there – both fascinating and appalling to the innocent eye:

An indescribable architecture, apparently of expediency, lends itself to the caprices of the ground, with a crowd of houses cut into points, in the form of triangular towers, of erect and overturned pyramids, surrounded with bridges, ditches, props, gathered together like the broken fragments of a mountain ... Constantinople is a Babylon, a world, a chaos.[4]

It took unexpected knowledge and a readiness to abandon western aesthetics to make coherent pictures in the face of such a visual and historical dislocation.

The most astonishing photography undertaken by the western photographers in the Near East grapples with cultural and physical extremes: too much or too little for conventional control. How to cope with whole unknown cultures, what to do with a landscape made of sand – it was a challenge of understanding and communication of a fascinating kind. Many of the photographers were 'reduced' to photographing 'nothing'. And in those photographs of 'nothing' they denied the western pictorial tradition. It is, in fact, disconcerting to find many pictures amongst these exploratory photographs which anticipate a modern aesthetic by more than half a century. Even more surprising is that contemporary criticism accepted, and even applauded these pictures.

As an example, Roger Fenton's key photograph taken during the Crimean War, *The Valley of the Shadow of Death* (fig 25), contains a slightly curved track over a low, undramatic hill overhung by a bald sky. In Fenton's own words, 'the sight passed all imagination: round shot and shell lay like a stream at the bottom of the hollow all the way down, you could not walk without treading on them.'[5] There is no other physical evidence of the horror and violence of the battle. The *Art Journal*, the main critical aesthetic periodical in Britain at the time, called this empty picture 'a most exquisite photograph'[6]

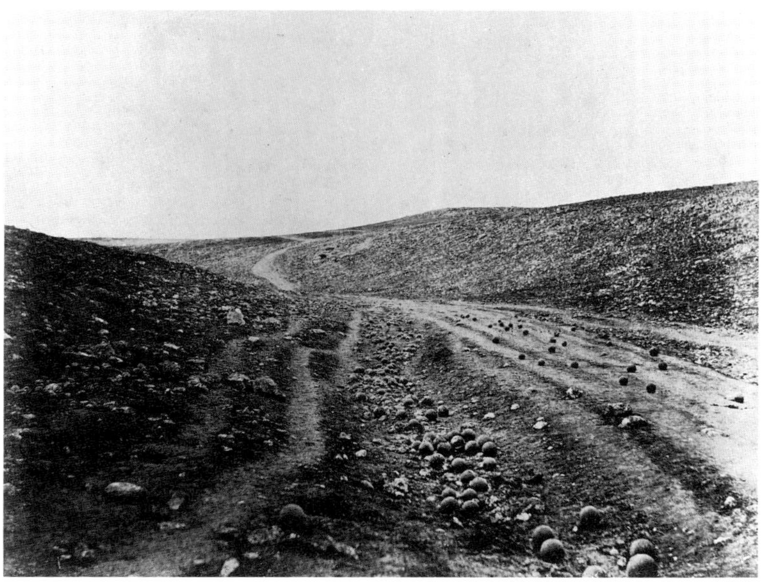

FIG 25 ROGER FENTON
The Valley of the Shadow of Death
1855 (Royal Photographic Society, Bath)

('exquisite' being understood in the sense of 'sharply painful'). That is to say, that Fenton's audience recognised the photograph for its cold, hard desolation, all the more poignant because there is no life there – not a blade of grass, not even the humanity of fallen bodies. It is an apt image of hell.

The rationale behind this idea of photographing desolation or nothingness may be said to come from the verbal tradition of the Bible. Fenton's title comes from Psalm 23 and conveys a message beyond the desolation that makes his a bearable picture after all, that makes it only an earthly picture of hell and a potential path to Christian salvation:

Yea, though I walk through the valley of the shadow of death, I will fear no evil: for thou art with me; thy rod and thy staff they comfort me. Thou preparest a table before me in the presence of mine enemies ...[7]

The metaphorical character of much of the Bible's teaching and the use of very simple, direct images would mean that the land, the stone, the very sands sang with familiar words in western ears. A mystical sense of the land and the need to know it through walking through it, which in Europe was part of nationalism, in the Near East would support and arouse mystical faith. The desert lands, the archaeological ruins engraved with languages lost to knowledge, were knowable as the fulfilment of prophecy:

Upon the land of my people shall come up thorns and briers; yea, upon all the houses of joy in the joyous city: Because the palaces shall be forsaken; the multitude of the city shall be left; the forts and towers shall be dens for ever, a joy of wild asses, a pasture of flocks. But the cormorant and the bittern shall possess it; the owl also and the raven shall dwell in it: and he shall stretch out upon it the line of confusion, and the stones of emptiness.[8]

It might be said that 'the line of confusion, and the stones of emptiness' are an inherent part of both the religious and the Romantic drive in the western approach to the Near East; and that here the 'realism' of photography fell heir to poetry.

Western educational tradition was based on a Classical, Greek or Roman, world: languages and ideas of common currency and understanding amongst men of education throughout the West. Set beside this, western religious tradition was based on the Near-Eastern Hebraic world. While education and faith were not in opposition, there was a torque, or stress in the relationship between the two because of the inherent cultural differences. The Protestant countries, moreover, developed a returning relationship to the Testaments and the Hebraic cultural standpoint in rejecting the iconic or, in their terms, the 'idolatrous' traditions of the Roman Catholic Church.

The common visual language in the West between the Roman Catholic and the Protestant countries had remained that based on the Classical tradition. This left the Protestant artists with the painful dilemma that the most important part of their practice – the direct expression of faith – was cut off from them. The solution was led by the Biblical use of metaphor – the underlying depth of meaning which lay in the sight of reality. By taking sight and a mental sounding of that reality, they could approach religion. As an example of the way this might have worked, the arbitrary presence of

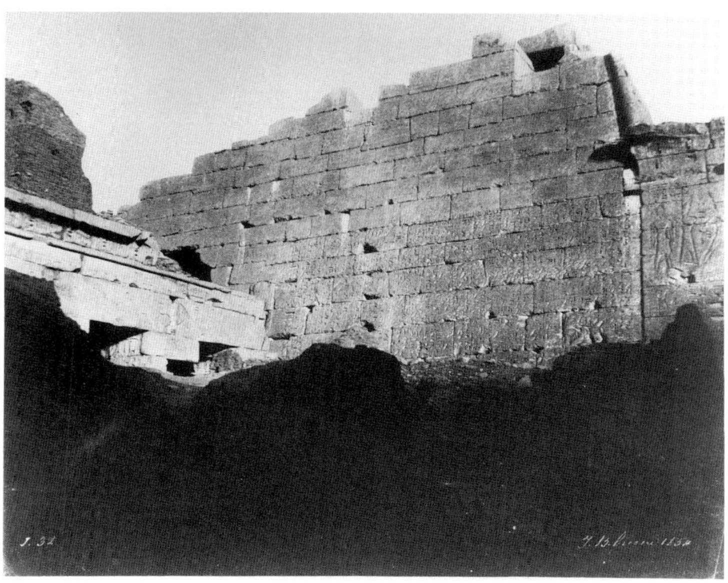

FIG 26 JOHN B. GREENE
Medinet Abu: Temple of Rameses III 1854
(Musée d'Orsay, Paris)

dark shadows in the photographs can be looked at in several ways. From the straightforward archaeological view to acquiring information, such pictures as John B. Greene's *Medinet Abu* (fig 26) are defective. Part of the information required is blocked off. At the simplest level, that is where the sun was when the photographer arrived.

At a level definable as an uncomplicated aesthetic interest in the extraordinary quality of light and shade in a new country, it may be the photographer enjoyed the effect. But a simple reaction does not prevent an additional, sophisticated reaction from following. It has been suggested that Greene may have thought of shadows in a melancholy sense – a sign of death – as a man sick of the illness that would soon kill him.[9]

There are, however, other possibilities. The word and idea of the shadow were not necessarily as gloomy as they were likely to be in countries such as Britain – shadow carries the idea of shelter from the vicious heat of the noon sun, preserving life:

Take counsel, execute judgment; make thy shadow as the night in the midst of the noonday; hide the outcasts; bewray not him that wandereth.[10]

In relation to Egypt, such a shadow finds a further echo in Isaiah's warning prophecy:

Woe to the rebellious children ... That walk down into Egypt, and have not asked at my mouth; to strengthen themselves in the strength of Pharaoh, and to trust in the shadow of Egypt. Therefore shall the strength of Pharaoh be your shame, and the trust in the shadow your confusion. For the Egyptians shall help in vain, and to no purpose: therefore have I cried concerning this, Their strength is to sit still.[11]

None of this is certain to Greene's picture but the photograph was taken by a Christian, working with these words in his head. The Christian photographers came to the Near East with a sense of mystery tied to the reality of the place. For them to take photographs not imbued with that mystery would be an eccentricity. For them to leave that mystery unexplained enabled the viewer to follow through the metaphor.

In straightforward aesthetic terms, the Near-Eastern landscape was a distinct challenge. Western pictorial rules would not work. In John B. Greene's Egyptian landscape photographs, there is an effective grasp of strangeness. His pictures, like the one of Gezireh (fig 27), simplify the landscape in a way that might have reduced their impact to nullity but in the event express the immense distances containing nothing, the floating mirage effect, which, for an island in the desert heat, is both reality and illusion.

Photographers, such as Greene, Félix Teynard and Maxime Du Camp, working with paper negatives and uncoated prints, had a medium particularly appropriate to catch monumental grandeur. The broad, blocked-out character of light and shade was radically different from, for example, the precise line drawing by Baron Dominique-Vivant Denon, which effectively reduces the impact of the monuments. The granular uncertainty of these photographs was not just true to the character of the stone, but, in expert hands, it has a density and richness which help to convey the physical atmosphere and give a sense of the shimmering life of the light.

Francis Frith encountered the same aesthetic

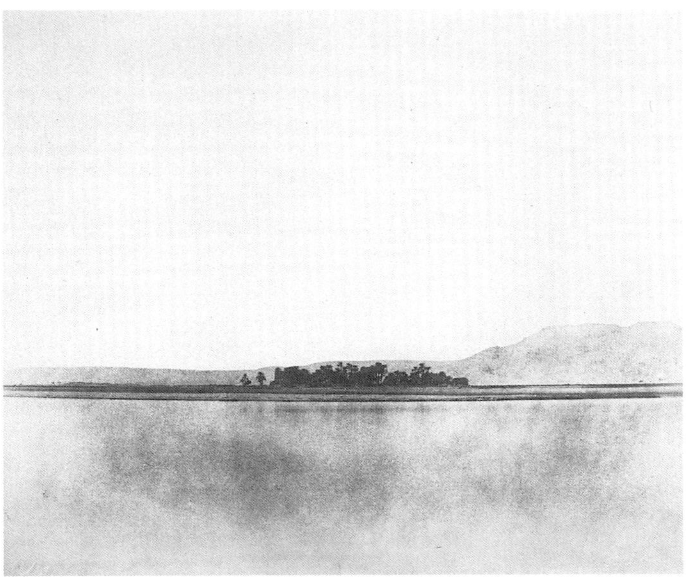

FIG 27 JOHN B. GREENE
Gezireh 1854
(Musée d'Orsay, Paris)

problem of a landscape with no foreground, no middle ground and an unfeatured sky:

... foregrounds are especially perverse; distance too near or too far ... some or all of these things (with plenty of others of a similar character) are the rule not the exception. I have often thought, when manoeuvring about for a position with my camera, of the exclamation of the mechanist of antiquity – 'give me a fulcrum for my lever, and I will move the world.'[12]

Unlike Greene, Frith was working with the detailed collodion process. He countered the problem with a geometric use of sand and masonry, identifying the fore- and middle grounds with human figures, sent to sit like map pins and make a place where there is none. In *The Pyramids of Sakkarah* (plate 31), dragged lines, like cycle tracks, become the essential visual relief.

From his commercial success, Frith might be seen as a straightforward businessman, whose self-deprecating comments on the practical difficulties of taking photographs in the desert are evidence of a simple, uncomplicated approach. But the beauty of his photographs is confirmed by his purely romantic words, an enthusiastic and poetic view of history:

The day and hour in a man's life upon which he first obtains a view of 'The Pyramids' is a time to date from for many a year to come; he is approaching, as it were, the presence of an immortality which has mingled vaguely with his thoughts from very childhood, and has been to him unconsciously an essential and beautiful form, and the most majestic mystery ever created by man.[13]

The feeling that comes from this passage is, unexpectedly for a convinced Quaker, a non-Christian concern. Beyond Classical education, beyond Christian faith, lay the Egyptian world. It could be coped with or organised into a progressive pattern by regarding it as a forerunner of the later civilisations – a historical 'attempt' to achieve order and superiority (a species of millennial imperialism). Frith's words, despite their reference to childhood, do not carry that implication.

A more explicit admiration comes in the text Félix Teynard wrote to accompany his Egyptian photographs: '*All the monuments which predate Alexander the Great are grand and profusely decorated; the forms are simple and the ornamentation is appropriate to their severe character: it is pure Egyptian architecture, which had developed naturally, without any foreign influence; it was the time of the pharaohs, it was the great Egyptian age.*'[14] This is reinforced by a following passage, which reads, '*The Christian age produced only ephemeral buildings; the temples were mutilated, degraded, turned into churches; the painted reliefs which decorated the walls were hammered, defaced, plastered and whitewashed over; the statues were smashed: it was a barbaric age.*'[15] Clearly, Teynard's ears were deaf to Biblical melancholy and more attuned to the French revolutionary approach to Egypt – seeking a cultural substitute for the Christian and Classical culture of the two upper 'estates': the clerics and the aristocracy.

Teynard was a civil engineer. This explains the background of his interest in such solid and unpicturesque structures as the rock-cut architecture of Beni Hasan; it does not explain the strength and originality of his pictures. The starting point of ideas is merely an indication of the direction they may take. It is a paradox that the kind of powerful directness and consistency of approach, with 'a secretarial neatness in conception and an extreme acuteness regarding scale and distance ... [and] a sense of intelligent measure',[16] which we might think characteristic of an engineer, belonged rather to the photographs taken by the poet, painter and journalist, Maxime Du Camp.

Teynard described his own photographs as taken 'to recall the feelings experienced during the many months we spent alone amongst the peoples of Egypt and Nubia.'[17] The physical experience of being in the Near East may fall under that heading of 'sensations' or feelings. The sense of being translated into a world where physical confidence is undermined and lost recurs throughout the artists' descriptions. Constraints and practical difficulties are a constant cry. Technical difficulties and unpredictable, fickle results were as striking as the aesthetic challenge. Sand engulfed the monuments, sand seeped into the processing – shifting the bulk to discover the subject and minutely filtering out the grains to protect the image were practical alternations of the general spirit of the experience – the overwhelming weight of the monuments and the focused fascination of details. The fierce control required to achieve results in quite phenomenally irritating circumstances is in itself a kind of historical virtue, adding heroism to the most prosaic vision. Creativity may be stimulated by the opposing conditions of constraint and freedom. Physical difficulties, from bandits to sunstroke, may nudge or drive the mind into unexpected paths.

Hallucinatory experiences are not simply the province of the opium smoker – consider Francis Frith in a small, tightly closed tent 1,000 miles from the mouth of the Nile with the thermometer registering 110°F and the collodion boiling on the glass plate of the negative[18] (collodion being a mixture of ether and unstabilised gun cotton). An unexpected physical experience could lead to an uncalculated or accidental lyricism. Sophia Poole's description of the Second Pyramid of El Geezeh, which accompanies Frith's photograph, explains the experience of climbing to the top:

... the casing remains from the summit for about a quarter of the distance to the base. On this account the ascent is a matter of great difficulty, and even danger, for when the traveller has gained the cased surface, he has not only exchanged steps for notches in the smooth stones, but he can see nothing between him and the ground, and he feels as though on a pyramid in the air.[19]

In the 1850s, the technical 'advance' of photography led to its development as a trade practised, suddenly, by thousands wearing the word 'artistic' happily in their hats. This caused an anxious withdrawal and a hostility to the idea of photography as capable of art amongst the painters. By 1857, Lady Eastlake's authoritative article on photography concluded that it was not capable of art. On the way to her conclusion, she makes some remarks which add an interesting gloss. The central problem was simple – the surprise had worn off:

... all things great and small, working together to produce what seemed at first as delightful, but as fabulous, as Aladdin's ring, which is now as little suggestive of surprise as our daily bread.[20]

It is, perversely, not knowledge that leads to this lack of surprise, but the comfortable ignorance bred from familiarity. Photography remained difficult, arbitrary and, in any broad sense, untruthful:

Photography is, after all, too profoundly interwoven with the deep things of Nature to be entirely unlocked by any given method ... all the certainty that the best of experience attains is, that you are dealing with one of those subtle agencies, which, though Ariel-like, will serve you bravely, will never be taught implicitly to obey.[21]

This sense of confusion is only arbitrarily resolved by her conclusion:

Her [photography's] business is to give evidence of facts as minutely and as impartially as, to our shame, only an unreasoning machine can give ... The millions and millions of hieroglyphs mentioned by M. Arago may be multiplied by millions and millions more, – she will render all as easily and as accurately as one.[22]

Eastlake was one of the great enthusiasts for photography in the 1840s. She is arguing here from a feeling that recurs in the industrial age, a feeling that she has been seduced by the cleverness of a toy into estimating its value too highly. There remain passages in the 1857 article in which she expresses some of that original affection:

There is no doubt that the forte of the camera lies in the imitation of one surface only, and that of a rough and broken kind. Minute light and shade, cognisant to the eye, but unattainable by hand, is its greatest and easiest triumph – the mere texture of stone, whether rough in the quarry or hewn on the wall, its especial delight ... if asked to say what photography has hitherto best succeeded in rendering, we should point to everything near and rough – from the texture of the worn sea-shell, of the rusted armour, and the fustian jacket, to those glorious architectural pictures of French, English, and Italian subjects, which, whether in quality, tone, detail, or drawing, leave nothing to be desired.[23]

Ironically, what she says here is Romantic in its concern and the opposite of the minute and impar-

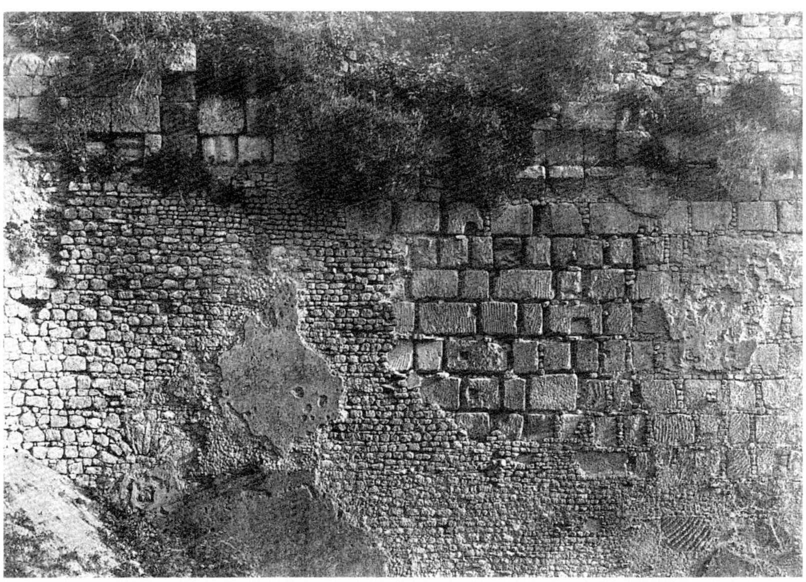

FIG 28
AUGUSTE SALZMANN
Jerusalem: The Walls of the Temple, Detail of the Probationary Pool 1854
(Musée d'Orsay, Paris)

tial examination of facts proposed in her conclusion. It is also no coincidence that she broke into poetic reference when talking about the technical defects of photography.

The odd idea that photographs of stone are the high point of aesthetic photography finds its justification in such photographs as Salzmann's picture of *The Walls of the Temple, Detail of the Probationary Pool* (fig 28). In a descriptive sense it is a wall in a state of decay, constructed of different bricks and stones. Archaeologically, it has a history, and it is this pre-eminently important history which provides the motive and the impetus behind the taking of pictures of this kind. In the context, the small, the modest, the little clues are loaded with potential meaning and mystery. The photographer was licensed to consider such pictures and to consider them as having greater weight than a pyramid or a colossus. Explaining why they are so astonishing and so beautiful, why so pleasing to the eye, is more difficult. Partly it is the unexpectedness: this is a new kind of picture to bear that degree of importance. It breaks the pictorial rules: no distance, no subject, no humanity. Partly it is the charm of paradox: it is a detail, not a whole, it does not explain itself. It is part of a whole series designed to make an archaeological argument, but, like the pivotal verse of a poem, stands by itself and takes on a private life, growing quietly like the little plants at the edge.[24]

Whatever the original intention behind these photographers' work, there is no simple impulse for factual truth. Salzmann's 'conclusive brutality' is off-centre, obscured by shadows, filled with plants covering the very stones he documents (plate 28); Teynard's Arabic stones are left to lean and obscure the carved words, and his accompanying text is a story not a history; Du Camp's figure of measurement, the man introduced to give scale, sits, so that we cannot even see how big he is, mockingly on the statue's head (plate 30). In practical terms we are left without the available data. The sheer perversity of this is evidence that the photographers are enjoying themselves – experimenting, breaking the rules – and the importance of their subject matter adds a most interesting weight of seriousness to their pleasure. This extraordinary fact is concealed by the occasional technical apology. But, in a world where shifting piles of sand and rubble were commonplace and archaeology still meant hacking out and carrying off anything that could be moved, the powerful delicacy of not stamping flat or weeding out little, obscuring plants has an inverted boldness that deserves deep respect.

It is notably disconcerting that photography, hailed as an accurate measuring and quantifying tool, was found to encompass an eccentric and accidental response liable to fall between the cracks of western culture – achieving effects that look strangely modern to our historical eye. The 'brutal' truth-teller that creates fictions is a contrary idea, but fit for an Orientalist romance – a western fiction based on a distant fact.

Notes and References

1 Elizabeth Eastlake, Review of the progress of photography, *Quarterly Review*, 1857, reprinted in *Photography: Essays and Images*, New York, 1981, p.86.

2 'Les photographies ne sont plus des récits, mais bien des faits doués d'une brutalité concluante.' Auguste Salzmann, Preface, *Jérusalem. Etude et réproduction photographique de la ville Sainte, depuis l'époque judaique jusqu'à nos jours*, 1856; Quoted in Françoise Heilbrun, 'Auguste Salzmann, photographe malgré lui', *F. de Saulcy 1807–1880 et la Terre Sainte*, Paris, Réunion des musées nationaux, 1982, p.118.

3 Sophia Poole or Reginald Poole, text for *Egypt, Sinai and Jerusalem, A series of twenty photographic views by Francis Frith*, London, 1860.

4 Edmondo de Amicis, *Constantinople*, quoted in Julie Lawson, *James Robertson of Istanbul*, London, 1991, p.21.

5 Roger Fenton, letter from Balaclava, 4 April 1855, quoted in Helmut & Alison Gernsheim, *Roger Fenton: Photographer of the Crimean War*, London, 1954, p.59.

6 'Photographs from Sebastopol', *Art Journal*, October 1855, p.285.

7 *Authorized King James Version of the Bible*, Psalm 23: 4–5.

8 Isaiah 32: 13–14, 34: 11.

9 Maria Morris Hambourg, *The Waking Dream. Photography's First Century*, New York, 1993, p.298.

10 Isaiah 16: 3.

11 Isaiah 30: 1–7.

12 Introduction, *Egypt and Palestine, Photographed and Described by F.Frith*, London, 1858–9.

13 Ibid., text for *The Sphinx and the Great Pyramid, El Geezeh.*

14 'Tous les monuments antérieurs à Alexandre le Grand sont grandioses, décorés avec profusion; les formes sont simples, et l'ornementation est en rapport avec le caractère sévère qui les distingue: c'est l'architecture égyptienne pure, qui s'est développée spontanément, sans influence étrangère; c'est l'époque pharaonique, c'est la belle époque.' Félix Teynard, *Egypte et Nubie. Sites et monuments les plus intéressants pour l'étude de l'art et de l'histoire*, Paris & London, 1858, pp.3–4.

15 'L'époque chrétienne ne produit que des constructions éphémères; les temples sont mutilés, dégradés, transformés en églises; les sculptures peintes qui décorent leur parois sont martelées, recouvertes d'enduits grossiers et de badigeon; les statues sont brisées: c'est une époque de barbarie.' Ibid.

16 André Jammes & Eugenia Parry Janis, *The Art of French Calotype*, Princeton, 1983, p.174.

17 'pour rémemorer les sensations éprouvées pendant les mois nombreux que nous avons passés, seul, au milieu des populations de l'Egypte et de la Nubie.' Teynard, op. cit.

18 Frith, op. cit.

19 Sophia Poole or Reginald Poole, op. cit.

20 Elizabeth Eastlake, op. cit., p.89.

21 Ibid, p.89.

22 Ibid, p.94.

23 Ibid, p.93.

24 'La photographie de détail, en les isolant de leur contexte, donne aux objets qu'elle reproduit, et dont elle accentue la présence d'une façon insolite, une vie propre, qui ouvre à nouveau le champ à l'imaginaire.' Françoise Heilbrun, op. cit., p.125.

James Robertson

B. A. and H. K. Henisch

JAMES ROBERTSON, the nineteenth-century photographer best known for his work in Istanbul and during the Crimean War, remains an elusive quarry for his admirers, but the outlines of his life are emerging slowly from the shadows.

Born in England, though probably of Scottish parentage, he spent most of his professional career in Istanbul, as Chief Engraver at the Imperial Mint. This appointment makes plausible the belief that he was the same Robertson who exhibited four medals at the Royal Academy in London, between 1833 and 1840. While still in England, he studied under William Wyon, who was Chief Engraver at the Royal Mint in London from 1828 onwards. When, round about 1840, the new sultan Abdulmejid decided to modernise the Imperial Mint in Istanbul, Robertson was one of several Europeans selected for the task, and his long career at the centre of the Ottoman Empire began in 1841. On 19 April 1855, he married the sister of Felice Beato, the man about to become his partner in a photographic business. This family connection doubtless explains the intrepid plan Robertson made for the last years of his life. Less than a fortnight after the farewell dinner given to honour him in Istanbul on his retirement from the Mint, on 29 October 1881, Robertson with his wife and three daughters embarked for Japan, to rejoin Beato, who had settled in Yokohama. Robertson died in Japan on 18 April 1888.

Set within the frame of this forty-year career as a medallist and engraver is a fifteen-year spell as an active photographer. There is evidence that Robertson enjoyed making sketches and water-colours, and with such tastes, together with his professional training, it is not surprising that he took up photography. From the first he seems to have thought of it as an occupation far more serious than a hobby, and to have sensed its potential for both fame and fortune. The earliest record of his work can be found in a diary entry for 4 July 1853, made by the Earl of Carlisle who, on that day of his visit to Istanbul, had just acquired some Robertson views. The last is of the photographic firm established by Robertson sometime later in Pera, the European quarter of the city. The company was still in business during the spring of 1867, but was put up for sale, with all its 'stock, goodwill, Apparatus and Negatives', in the autumn of that year.

An earlier traveller from England, the journalist Albert Smith, found a daguerreotype studio in Pera (Beyoglu), and had his portrait made there on 25 September 1849. Far more significant, Ernest de Caranza, a French engineer, came, like Robertson, to work on one of the sultan's many programmes to modernise the city, and produced two series of photographs in 1852 and 1854. In the small, intimate circle of expatriates, the two men must have met; indeed, some of their studies of buildings are taken from the same viewpoint. When Ernest Lacan wrote his review of the photography section of the 1855 Exposition Universelle in Paris, he bracketed the pair together for their achievement in bringing the beauties of Istanbul to the attention of their European admirers.

By mid-century, photography had thus found a foothold even in that sleepy, fabled capital of the Ottoman Empire, and Robertson sensed the possibilities of the place and the moment. The city sat at the crossroads of Europe and Asia, of the old and the new. By this time it was linked to Western Europe by a regular, weekly steamship service. It was possible to send despatches to the journals of Paris and London, and to read their recent issues in the heart of Pera. Fate had placed Robertson in a region of spiritual significance and strategic importance for the West. Travellers and armchair travellers alike were hungry for news and views of hallowed Christian sites and Greek antiquities, and were fascinated by the glamour and mystery of Islam. The area had also become a cockpit of international politics, and so there was another, wider public with a very practical interest in the clash of Great Powers as they fished in troubled waters for influence and advantage.

Robertson set out to feed these appetites, making enterprising and imaginative efforts to bring his work to the attention of an international public. He knew well enough that reputations are not quickly made from images kept in portfolios, and he made sure that his photographs were presented to the world through several channels. His first known album, *Photographic Views of Constantinople*, was published by Joseph Cundall in London in December 1853 and, in the course of that winter, patrons such as Prince Albert could select prints at the Photographic Institution in Bond Street. It may be that Robertson had established his firm as early as 1854, because another album, *Grecian Antiquities*, was issued in that year with the imprint: 'Published by the Photographic Establishment, Pera of Constantinople'.

His photographs reached a wider public in the form of engravings. The illustrated journals, established throughout Europe in the early 1840s, welcomed contributions from far-flung correspondents. In an October 1853 issue, the *Illustrated London News* published an engraving from a photograph by Robertson, 'Gate of Dolmabahçe Palace under construction', and for several years following the pages of that journal, and such counterparts as *Illustration Journal Universel* of Paris, or *Faust, Poligraphisch Illustrierte Zeitschrift* of Vienna, were sprinkled with his sketches and photographs.

Engraved versions of Robertson's photographic studies also found their way into albums and printed books. For travellers to and from the East, Trieste was an important junction, where the railways met the steamers of the Austrian-Lloyd shipping company. This firm published in about 1854 an attractive album, *Souvenirs de Constantinople*, specially designed for an international clientele, with three languages, French, German and English represented on the title-page. The album contains no text, just twenty-eight captioned engravings, of which twenty-one are labelled 'Photographie von Robertson'.

One photograph could provide material for different engravers, working for different publishers. On 10 June 1854, the *Illustrated London News* carried an advertisement for the English translation of Théophile Gautier's travel memoir, *Constantinople of Today*. Inside the book was printed this acknowledgement: 'The engravings that illustrate this volume have been copied from Photographic Pictures by Robertson, kindly lent for this purpose by the Proprietors of the Photographic Institution.' It is possible to compare one Robertson print with the engraving made from it for *Souvenirs de Constantinople*, and with the version that appeared in *Constantinople of Today* (figs 29, a, b and c).

A formal exhibition offered any artist a natural forum, and the long, leisurely reviews that described it brought some knowledge of the exhibitors and their approach to readers unable to walk through the rooms and see for themselves. Robertson's views were shown on at least six occasions in London, Paris and Manchester, between December 1854 and 1860. It soon became possible for anyone really interested in travel photographs not merely to read

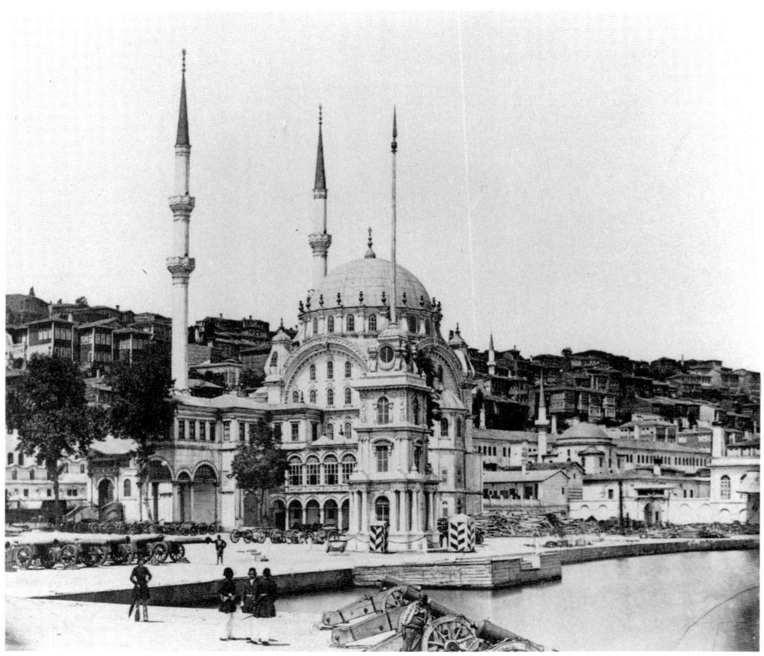

FIG 29 A–C
left to right:

A JAMES ROBERTSON
Mosque of Sultan Mahmud at Tophana c.1854.
(Science Museum, London)

B *Mosque of Sultan Mahmud at Tophana* from Théophile Gautier, *The Constantinople of Today*, London, 1854

C *Mosque of Sultan Mahmud at Tophana* from *Souvenirs de Constantinople*, Trieste, c.1854

about them but to acquire a selection by subscribing to one of several societies that sent out parcels of approved photographs at regular intervals. Far away in Australia, the trustees of the recently established State Library of Victoria obtained, in 1860, a considerable body of images of the Near East and the Mediterranean region, including many by Robertson, by taking out a subscription to the London Architectural Photographic Association.

During his years as an active photographer he made forays into Greece, Malta, the Holy Land, Egypt and Damascus. All Robertson's surviving prints of landscape or architectural details were made in Istanbul itself or in the vicinity of the major stopping points for travellers along the Mediterranean steamship routes. Indeed, because travel into the interior was still difficult at that time, artists and photographers, like tourists in general, had little option but to rely on local guides and stick to the beaten track.

Circumstance made Robertson a western artist in the Ottoman world; chance transformed him for a while into that new creature, a war photographer. For the Crimean War, which began for Britain on 27 March 1854, Robertson found himself at the ideal vantage point. The main war zone was the Black Sea and the Crimean peninsula; Scutari (Uskudar), just across from Istanbul, on the opposite bank of the Bosphorus, was chosen as the British staging post and hospital area. Robertson was quick to seize the moment. He photographed several regimental groups after they disembarked at Scutari, in the months of May and June, and reproductions of pictures appeared a little later in the *Illustrated London News*. Unlike his more famous rival, Roger Fenton, who made the long journey from Britain to the Crimea only once, in the spring of 1855, Robertson was able to go to and fro easily, because the voyage from Istanbul to Balaclava, the main British camp on the peninsula, took only two days. It is certain that Robertson was photographing in the Crimea on at least two occasions in the early summer of 1855, and in the autumn of that year. There are also Robertson photographs which record the last groups of British soldiers to leave the Crimea, in the summer of 1856. As it is unlikely that Robertson would be given leave of absence from his duties at the Mint for so many months, it seems probable that he made several short expeditions rather than one long visit to the battlefront.

Robertson took pains to ensure for his war photographs the widest possible publicity. They were displayed at exhibitions in London from December 1855 right through the following year, and some were selected for the Manchester Art Treasures Exhibition in 1857. They were published as engravings, and it is possible that a few were also issued as stereo cards. The Crimean pictures which made Robertson's reputation were all taken in the aftermath of war, as sobering testimony to the chaos created by battle, sombre views of military burial grounds, or records of the mining operations carried out by British engineers to destroy the Russian dockyards at Sebastopol.

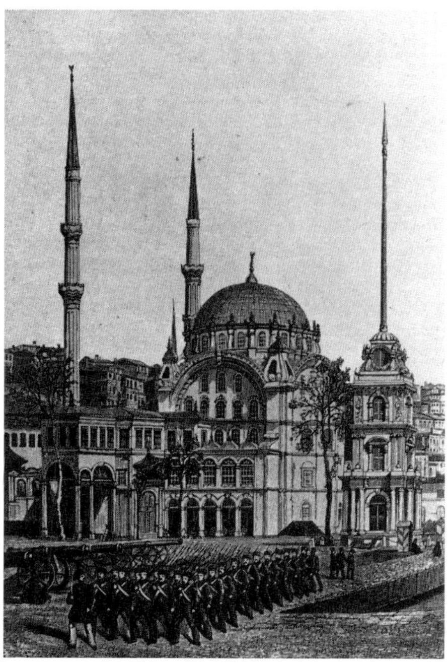

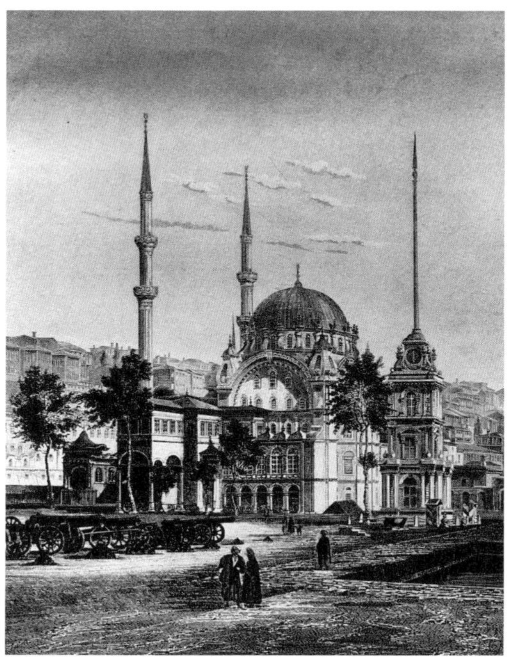

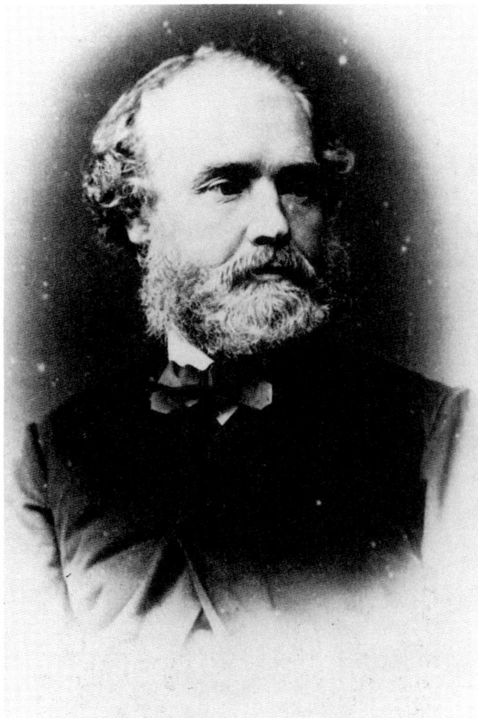

FIG 30 ABDULLAH FRERES
Carte-de-visite portrait of James Robertson c.1868
(Courtesy of Bahattin Öztuncay)

About Robertson, the private man, there are few clues. A carte-de-visite portrait, *c.*1868 (fig 30), shows a handsome, well-groomed man. In a handful of references he is remembered as a genial dinner companion. Alexis Soyer, the great chef, for example, fondly recalled the occasion in Marseille when he and Robertson 'once more degustated the celebrated bouillabaisse'. There is one disturbing glimpse of a darker side to his character, when he broke a gentleman's agreement with M. J. Diness, the Jewish photographer in Jerusalem, by taking advantage of this rival's local knowledge and stealing some of his business.

About Robertson, the artist, there is more to be said. In his war reportage, he was something of a pioneer, although he may have modelled his approach in part on the sketches of fortifications and battle terrains which had long been made by military men with a trained eye and a practical pencil.

For his main achievement, the views of an exotic world, filled with extraordinary buildings and peopled with picturesque inhabitants, he laboured in a well-defined tradition, for which there were already many guideposts. He, and discriminating contemporary viewers, must have measured his images, inevitably, by the only yardstick available, the work of the Orientalist painters. Ernest Lacan, the critic, explicitly compared Robertson to Alexandre-Gabriel Decamps (1803–60), commissioned by the French government to paint such scenes. Artists paid leisurely visits to Istanbul, and some, such as Amadeo, Count Preziosi (1816–82), settled there for many years, to produce pictures of its people and scenery for western residents and travellers. In the tightly knit European community, it was possible to make friendships and exchange views. The second surviving portrait of Robertson shows him with Fabius Brest (1823–1900), a French painter who spent four productive years in Istanbul, from 1855 to 1859. Robertson's own sketches and watercolours reveal his artist's eye for the possibilities of the marvellous city in the years just before he began to experiment with photography. The engraved frontispiece of Albert Smith's travel book, *A Month in Constantinople* (1850), is based on 'a charming watercolour sketch' by Mr Robertson of the Mint (fig 31). It shows 'The Shoe Bazaar', in which the everyday, prosaic realities of shopping have been transformed for Western eyes into an enchanted scene straight out of the *Arabian Nights.*

As a photographer, Robertson rarely placed men and women in this way in the foreground of his compositions. Attention is concentrated on a building and its surroundings; his landscape is peopled by small figures, used not for their own sake but to enliven the scene, to add a sense of scale or a piquant contrast between picturesque clothes and monumental architecture, life's brevity and the enduring beauty of great buildings. In only one branch of his work did Robertson give prominence to the human figure, and that was in his popular line of 'types', impersonal studies of the people who bustled through the streets of Istanbul, engaged in a thousand different kinds of activity (fig 32). Robertson was well known to his contemporaries for such portraits. Lacan regretted that the photographer had sent no examples to the Exposition Universelle in 1855, and chided him for depriving the public by this oversight much pleasure and information. Actual Robertson photographs in this genre are now hard to find, although a few are preserved in other forms. The frontispiece of Walter Thornbury's *Turkish Life and Character* (1860) shows a street porter, engraved from a Robertson image. The photographs which survive are sometimes hand-tinted, possibly by Robertson himself, who was well equipped to act as his own colourist. Such photographic studies of characteristic costumes and occupations were heirs to a long pictorial tradition. Colour added to their charm, and helped the subdued, monochrome originals to compete with the brilliance of the tinted lithographs and engravings which were already familiar to the potential customer.

There was in Robertson's make-up as an artist a certain documentary streak. This shows itself most often in his Crimean War work, but it surfaces occasionally in his other studies, for example in that 1853 photograph of the 'Gate of Dolmabachçe Palace under Construction' which, as already mentioned, he sent to the *Illustrated London News*. In the main, though, he tried to give the viewer not the gritty reality of contemporary conditions, but an idealised and distanced distillation of the daily scene. The filth and evidence of disease in the streets of Near Eastern cities, so graphically described by appalled western travellers, are nowhere to be found in Robertson's pictures. Great ruins in Greece may be surrounded by disorder or debris, but the desolation is handled with decorum, seen always from a safe distance. It does not disgust the spectator, but intensifies the melancholy beauty of the view. The crumbling glories of the past are not studied in isolation, but stand like ancient giants stranded in an alien world. The glittering façade of a palace in Istanbul is shown not as a pristine architectural model, but as a backdrop to the busy lives of knife-grinders and porters, so used to its familiar presence that they no longer see, let alone marvel at, its subtle splendours.

Although Robertson was employed to modernise the Mint, and although his photographs show the contemporary scene, he was not inspired by contemporary improvements. The sultan who ruled later in the century, Abdulhamid II, commissioned photographs as records of progress and modern developments throughout his vast empire. Schools, hospitals, military installations, all figure prominently in the official albums he compiled for presentation to western heads of state. Robertson's pictures belong to an older tradition, and offer no hint of change, or any wish for it. In its place, the modern camera reveals a timeless world, the marvels of the East, caught in the kaleidoscope of western dreams. Robertson, the man of business, might pay lip-service to the march of progress, but Robertson the photographer sensed that his viewers wanted pictures to be windows, opening out from the prose of life onto the playground of the imagination.

As a long-term resident, Robertson came to know the Ottoman world intimately, but his eye always retained the freshness of a stranger's first response. Like the Orientalist painters, he remained alert to the charm of exotic costumes in extraordinary situations. His camera loved to linger on the beauty of bold contours and ethereal lattice-work, modelled by the ever-changing play of light and shadow. In the characteristic Robertson image, the mundane and the majestic are interlaced, inseparable, each element essential for the whole effect. The settings are serene, but within them the myriad small dramas of daily life are played out against a noble background of past glory, present grandeur.

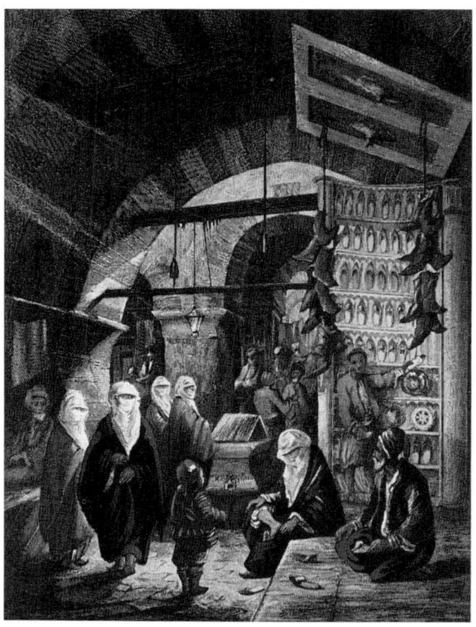

FIG 31 AFTER JAMES ROBERTSON
The Shoe Bazaar from Albert Smith, *A Month in Constantinople*, London, 1850

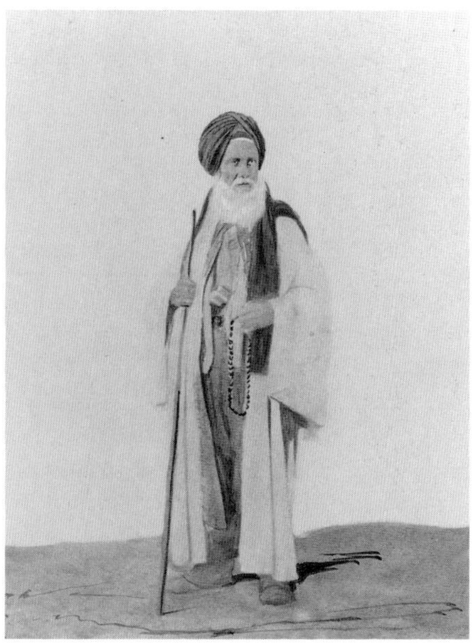

FIG 32 JAMES ROBERTSON
Mullah c.1850
(Courtesy of Bahattin Öztuncay)

Select Bibliography

Ackerman, Gerald, *Les Orientalistes de l'Ecole Brittanique,* Paris, 1991

Ahmed, Leila, *Edward W. Lane: A study of his life and works and of British ideas of the Middle East in the nineteenth century,* London and New York, 1978

Alderidge, Patricia, *Richard Dadd,* London, 1974

Allen, W. 'The Abdul Hamid II Collection', *History of Photography,* vol.8, no.2, pp.119–43

Ballantine, James, *The Life of David Roberts R.A., compiled from his Journals and Other Sources,* Edinburgh, 1866

Barber, Noel, *Lords of the Golden Horn,* London, 1973

Bendiner, Kenneth Paul, 'The Portrayal of the Middle East in British Painting 1835–1860' Ph.D. dissertation, Columbia University, 1979

The Bible, King James Authorised Version

Borcoman, James, *The Painter as Photographer: D. O. Hill, Auguste Salzmann, Charles Nègre,* Vancouver Art Gallery, 1978

Brown, David Blayney, *Sir David Wilkie: Drawings and Sketches in the Ashmolean Museum,* Ashmolean Museum, University of Oxford, 1985

Byron, Lord George, *Poetical Works,* Oxford, 1970

Byron, Exhibition Catalogue, Victoria and Albert Museum, London, 1974

Campbell, Dr J. P., 'David Wilkie', unpublished Ph.D. Thesis, University of Edinburgh, 1979

Clark, Kenneth, *The Nude,* London, 1956

Clark, Kenneth, *The Romantic Rebellion,* London, 1976

Clayton, Peter A., *The Rediscovery of Ancient Egypt,* London, 1982

Cook, E. T. and Wedderburn, A., *The Works of John Ruskin,* London, 1903–12

Cunningham, Allan, *The Life of Sir David Wilkie with his Journals, Tours, and Critical Remarks on Works of Art and a Selection from his Correspondence,* London, 1843

Dawson, Warren R. and Uphill, Eric P., *Who Was Who in Egyptology,* The Egypt Exploration Society, London, 1972

Denon, Baron Dominque-Vivant, *Description de l'Égypte,* 23 vols., Paris, 1808–29

Eastlake, Lady Elizabeth, *Photography: Essays and Images,* New York, 1881

Edwards, Gary, 'Photographs of Greece in the Musée d'Orsay's Album of the Duc de Chartres', *History of Photography,* vol.14, no.2, 1990, pp.165–79

Errington, Lindsay, *Tribute to Wilkie,* National Galleries of Scotland Catalogue, 1985

Ettinghausen, Richard, *Turkish Miniatures from the Thirteenth to the Eighteenth Century,* Milan, 1965

Evans, Joan, *The Lamp of Beauty: Writings on art by John Ruskin,* Oxford, 1980

Exhibition catalogue, *A Middle-Eastern Journey: Artists on their Travels, from the Collection of Rodney Searight,* Talbot Rice Art Centre, Edinburgh, and Sainsbury Centre for the Visual Arts, Norwich 1980–1

Exhibition catalogue, *Eastern Encounters: Orientalist Painters of the Nineteenth Century,* The Fine Art Society, 1978

Exhibition catalogue, *The Pre-Raphaelites,* Tate Gallery, 1984

Exhibition catalogue, *Travellers Beyond the Grand Tour,* The Fine Art Society, 1980

Exhibition catalogue, *Romantic Lebanon, The European View 1700–1900,* Leighton House Gallery, 1986

Exhibition catalogue, *The Pre-Raphaelites,* Tate Gallery, 1984

Exhibition catalogue, *L'Orientalisme dans les collections des Musées de Tours,* Musée des Beaux Arts, Tours, 1980

Exhibition catalogue, *The Inspiration of Egypt: its influence on British Artists, Travellers and Designers, 1700–1900,* Brighton Museum and Manchester City Art Gallery, 1983

Exhibition catalogue, *The Image of the Turk in Europe,* Metropolitan Museum of Art, New York, 1973

Exhibition catalogue, *Les Orientalistes provinçaux,* Musée des Beaux Arts, Marseille, 1982–3

Exhibition catalogue, Stevens, Mary Ann, *The Orientalists: Delacroix to Matisse,* Royal Academy of Arts, London, 1984

Exhibition catalogue, *Sir David Wilkie of Scotland (1785–1841),* Raleigh, North Carolina, 1987

Forster, E. S., trans., *The Turkish Letters of Ogier de Busbecq, Imperial Ambassador at Constantinople 1554–1562,* Oxford, 1968

Frith, Francis, *Egypt, Sinai and Jerusalem. A Series of Twenty Photographic Views, With descriptions by Mrs Sophia Poole and Reginald Stuart Poole,* London, 1858

Frith, Francis, *Egypt and Palestine, Photographed and Described,* London, 1858–1859

Gallichon, E. M., *Gérôme, peintre ethnographe,* Gazette des Beaux Arts, 1ère période, XXIV, February, 1868

Gardiner, Sir Alan, *Egypt of the Pharaohs,* Oxford, 1961

Gernsheim, Helmut and Alison, *Roger Fenton Photographer of the Crimean War,* London, 1954

Goncourt, Edmund and Jules, *French Eighteenth Century Painters,* Oxford, 1981

Goodall, Frederick, *The Reminiscences of Frederick Goodall RA,* London, 1902

Greene, John B., *Le Nil – Monuments – Paysages – Explorations photographiques,* Lille, 1854

Greene, John B. *Fouilles executées à Thebes dans l'année 1855: textes hieroglyphiques et documents inédits,* Paris, 1855

Guiterman, Helen, *David Roberts R.A. 1796–1864,* London, 1978

Guiterman, H. and Llewellyn, B., *David Roberts,* Barbican Art Gallery Catalogue, London, 1986

Hambourg, Maria Morris, Apraxine, Pierre, et al, *The Waking Dream, Photography's first Century,* New York, 1993

Hannavy, John, *Roger Fenton of Crimble Hall,* London, 1975

Heilbrun, Françoise, 'Auguste Salzmann, photographe malgré lui,' *F. de Saulcy 1807–1880 et la Terre Sainte,* Paris, Réunion des musées nationaux, 1982

Henisch, B. A. & H. K., 'Robertson of Constantinople', *Image,* vol.17, no.3, 1974, pp.1–9

Henisch, B. A. & H. K., 'James Robertson of Constantinople; a Chronology', *History of Photography,* vol.14, no.1, 1990, pp.23–32

de Herdt, Anne, *Dessins de Liotard*, Geneva and Paris, 1992

Holman Hunt, William, *Pre-Raphaelitism and the Pre-Raphaelite Brotherhood*, London, 1905

Hyman, Susan, *Edward Lear in the Levant: Travels in Albania, Greece and Turkey in Europe 1848–9*, London, 1988

Irwin, David and Francesca, *Scottish Painters at Home and Abroad*, London, 1975

Jammes, André, and Janis, Eugenia Parry, *The Art of the French Calotype*, Princeton, 1983

Jammes, Bruno, 'John B. Greene, an American Calotypist' *History of Photography* 5, no.4, pp.305–24

Johnson, Lee, *The Paintings of Eugène Delacroix: A Critical Catalogue 1816–1831*, Oxford, 1981

Julian, Phillippe, *The Orientalists, European Painters of Eastern Scenes*, Oxford, 1977

Kaplan, Fred, *Thomas Carlyle, A Biography*, Cambridge, 1983

Lacan, Ernest, *Esquisses Photographiques à propos de l'Exposition Universelle*, Paris, 1856, repr. Arno Press Inc, New York, 1979, pp.105–211

Lane, Edward William, *Manners and Customs of the Modern Egyptians*, 1836, reprinted 1989

Lawrence, A. W., *The Travel Letters of Lady Mary Wortley Montagu*, London, 1930

Lawson, Julie, 'James Robertson of Istanbul', essay in the catalogue of an exhibition organised by the British Council, in association with the Scottish National Portrait Gallery, Edinburgh. British Council, London, 1991

Lewis, Major-General Michael, *John Frederick Lewis, RA*, Leigh-on-Sea, 1978

Llewellyn, Briony, *The Orient Observed: Images of the Middle East from the Searight Collection*, Victoria and Albert Museum, 1989

Lloyd, Valerie, *Roger Fenton, Photographer of the 1850s*, Hayward Gallery, London, 1988

Lockhart, John Gibson, *Peter's Letters to his Kinsfolk*, ed. William Ruddick, Edinburgh, 1977

McKay, Agnes Ethel, *Arthur Melville, Scottish Impressionist (1855–1904)*, Leigh-on-Sea, 1951

Murphy, Dervla, *Embassy to Constantinople, The Travels of Lady Mary Wortley Montagu*, London, 1988

Nash, Joseph, *Sir David Wilkie's Sketches in Turkey, Syria, and Egypt 1840–1 drawn on stone*, London, 1843

Newhall, Beaumont, *The History of Photography*, (revised edition), New York, 1982

Newhall, Beaumont, 'John Beasely Greene 1832–1856' *Untitled*, Carmel, no.25, 1981, pp. 33–40

Noakes, Vivien, *Edward Lear: the Life of a Wanderer*, London, 1968

Nochlin, Linda, 'The Imaginary Orient', *Art in America*, May 1963, vol.71

Ormond, L. and R., *Lord Leighton*, New Haven and London, 1975

Osman, Colin, 'The Later Years of James Robertson', *History of Photography*, vol.16, no.1, 1992, pp.72–3

Öztuncay, Bahattin, 'Ernest de Caranza', *History of Photography*, vol.15, no.2, 1991, pp.139–43

Öztuncay, Bahattin, *James Robertson, Pioneer of Photography in the Ottoman Empire*, Istanbul, 1992

Palmer, Alan, *The Decline and Fall of the Ottoman Empire*, London, 1992

Pare, Richard, *Photography and Architecture*, Montreal, 1982

Quennell, Peter, *Byron, A Self-Portrait, Letters and Diaries 1798–1824*, Oxford, 1990

Roberts, David, *The Holy Land, Syria, Idumea, Arabia, Egypt and Nubia*, 6 vols, London, 1842–9

Romer, John, *Valley of the Kings*, London, 1981

Ruskin, John, *Academy Notes*, 1904

Rutherford, Andrew, *Byron, The Critical Heritage*, London, 1970

Said, Edward, *Orientalism*, New York, 1978

Searight, Sarah, *The British in the Middle East*, London, 1979

Seddon, John B., *Memoirs and Letters of the late Thomas Seddon, by his Brother*, New York, 1972

Sim, Katharine, *David Roberts R.A. 1796–1864, A Biography*, London, 1984

Sobieszk, Robert, 'Auguste Salzmann, Photographer,' *Image 14*, no.4–5, December 1971

Staley, Alan, *The Pre-Raphaelite Landscape*, Oxford, 1973

Steegmuller, F., ed., *Flaubert in Egypt*, Chicago, 1979

Stevenson Smith, W., *The Art and Architecture of Ancient Egypt*, Harmondsworth and New York, 1958

Stewart, J., trans., *Eugène Delacroix: Selected Letters 1813–1863*, London, 1971

Strachey, Lady, ed., *Letters of Edward Lear*, London, 1907

Sweetman, John, *The Oriental Obsession*, Cambridge, 1988

Teynard, Félix, *Egypte et Nubie, Sites et Monuments, les plus intéressants pour l'étude de l'art et de l'histoire*, Paris and London, 1858

Félix Teynard Calotypes of Egypt, A Catalogue Raisonné, essay by Kathleen Stewart Howe, New York, London and Carmel, 1992 (This publication reprints Teynard's text.)

Thackeray, W. M., *Notes of a Journey from Cornhill to Grand Cairo*, published in *Works*, London, 1900

Thompson, James, *The East Imagined, Experienced, Remembered. Orientalist Nineteenth-Century Painting*, National Gallery of Ireland and National Museums and Galleries on Merseyside, 1988

Thornton, Lynne, *The Orientalists, Painter-Travellers 1828–1908*, Paris, 1983

Tidrick, Kathryn, *Heart Beguiling Araby, The English Romance with Arabia*, London, 1981

Tillet, The Rev Leslie Selwyn, *Egypt itself*, 1984

Vaczek, Louis and Buckland, Gail, *Travellers in Ancient Lands: A Portrait of the Middle East 1839–1919*, New York, 1981

Vercoutter, Jean, trans. Sharman, Ruth, *The Search for Ancient Egypt*, London and New York, 1986

Wood, Christopher, *Dictionary of Victorian Painters*, 1971

Lenders to the Exhibition

Aberdeen Art Gallery and Museums

Agnew's, London

Ashmolean Museum, Oxford

Birmingham Museums and Art Gallery

Bradford Art Galleries and Museums

British Library, London

British Museum, London

Courtauld Institute Galleries, London

Fitzwilliam Museum, Cambridge

Forbes Magazine Collection, New York

Glasgow Art Gallery and Museum, Kelvingrove

Guildhall Art Gallery, London

Harris Museum and Art Gallery, Preston

King's College, Cambridge

Musée du Louvre, Paris

Musée d'Orsay, Paris

Musée du Petit Palais, Paris

National Gallery, London

National Gallery of Scotland, Edinburgh

National Library of Scotland, Edinburgh

National Museum of Photography, Film and Television, Bradford

National Museums of Scotland, Edinburgh

National Portrait Gallery, London

Orleans House Gallery, Twickenham

Royal Academy of Arts, London

Royal Scottish Academy, Edinburgh

Sheffield City Art Galleries

Tate Gallery, London

Victoria and Albert Museum, London

The Earl of Wemyss and March

Whitworth Art Gallery, University of Manchester

Williamson Art Gallery and Museum, Birkenhead

Private Collections

Exhibition Checklist

Sir William Allan

The Bride of Abydos
1836
Oil on canvas
60.9 × 47 cm
On loan from Glasgow Museums and Art Gallery

The Slave Market, Constantinople
1838
Oil on panel
129 × 198 cm
National Gallery of Scotland, Edinburgh

A Turkish Soldier on Horseback
1815
Watercolour over pencil on paper
34.8 × 26.6 cm
National Gallery of Scotland, Department of Prints and Drawings, Edinburgh

Haslan Gheray conducting Alkazia, the Daughter of Mouradin Bey across the Kuban
1817
Oil on panel
87 × 70 cm
On loan from the Earl of Wemyss and March

A Circassian Chief Selling to a Turkish Pacha Captives of a Neighbouring Tribe Taken in War
1815
Oil on panel
81.5 × 122.5 cm
On loan from the Earl of Wemyss and March

Francis Arundale

Ruins of a Temple: Entrance to the Temple of Hathor, Denderah
c.1823–33
Watercolour on paper
26.5 × 18.5 cm
On loan from the British Library, London

Capitals at Philae
c.1823–33
Watercolour on paper
21 × 30.5 cm
On loan from the British Library, London

Sir William Beechey

Thomas Hope
1798
Oil on canvas
221.6 × 168.9 cm
On loan from the National Portrait Gallery, London

Attributed to Gentile Bellini

The Sultan Mehmet II
1480 (?)
Oil on canvas
69.9 × 52.1 cm
On loan from the Trustees of the National Gallery, London

Giovanni Battista Belzoni

Narrative of the Operations and Recent Discoveries within the Pyramids ... in Egypt and Nubia
Published 1820
On loan from the National Library of Scotland, Edinburgh

Attributed to Joseph Bonomi

Wall Painting from a Tomb in the Valley of the Kings
c.1830
Coloured inks on paper
40 × 32.5 cm
On loan from the British Library, London

Wall Painting
c.1830
Coloured inks on paper
45 × 33 cm
On loan from the British Library, London

Sam Bough

Oriental Scene
Undated
Watercolour on paper
23 × 32.7 cm
On loan from the Board of Trustees of the Victoria and Albert Museum, London (Searight Collection)

Julia Margaret Cameron

Thomas Carlyle
1867
Albumen print
33.5 × 28 cm
On loan from the National Museum of Photography, Film and Television, Bradford

William Holman Hunt
1864
Albumen print
26.3 × 21.3 cm
On loan from the National Museum of Photography, Film and Television, Bradford

Maxime Du Camp

Abu Simbel: West Colossus of the Façade
1852
Blanquard-Evrard print
21.9 × 16.1 cm
On loan from the Royal Photographic Society, Bath

Relief Sculpture on Exterior of Temple of Karnak
Published 1852
Blanquard-Evrard print
16.2 × 20.9 cm
On loan from the Royal Photographic Society, Bath

Temple at Denderah: Reliefs on the Rear Facade
Published 1852
Blanquard-Evrard print
15.7 × 21.9 cm
On loan from the Royal Photographic Society, Bath

Great Temple at Denderah
Published 1852
Blanquard-Evrard print
16.1 × 21.9 cm
On loan from the Royal Photographic Society, Bath

Flaubert in the Garden of the Hotel du Nil, Cairo
1850
Blanquard-Evrard print
On loan from the Board of Trustees of the Victoria and Albert Museum, London

Attributed to Frederick Catherwood

Excavations at the Memnonium, Thebes
1831–3
Camera lucida drawing on paper
27 × 37 cm
On loan from the British Library, London

Medinet Abu
1831–3
Camera lucida drawing with wash on paper
18.5 × 27 cm
On loan from the British Library, London

Ruins – Excavation at Medinet Abu
1831–3
Camera lucida drawing in pencil on paper
27 × 37.5 cm
On loan from the British Library, London

Charles-Nicolas Cochin the Elder

The Masked Ball in the Grand Gallery at Versailles
1745
Line engraving
48 × 76.5 cm
On loan from the Trustees of the British Museum

Richard Dadd

Six drawings from a sketchbook
1842–3
Pencil on paper
14 × 20.5 cm (sheet size)
On loan from the Board of Trustees of the Victoria and Albert Museum, London

Sir Thomas Phillips in Eastern Costume, reclining with a Hookah
1842
Watercolour heightened with white on paper
17.8 × 25.4 cm
None
On loan from Agnew's, London

Self-Portrait
c.1841
Oil on panel
54.6 × 43.2 cm
On loan from a Private Collection

View in Rhodes
1845 (?)
Watercolour on paper
24.3 × 37.1 cm
On loan from the Board of Trustees of the Victoria and Albert Museum, London

Alexandre-Gabriel Decamps

The Duel
1827–8 (?)
Watercolour on paper
30 × 39.5 cm
On loan from the Board of Trustees of the Victoria and Albert Museum, London (Searight Collection)

Eugène Delacroix

Two Oriental Horsemen in Combat
Undated
Pencil on paper
33.5 × 22.4 cm
On loan from the Musée du Louvre, Departément des Arts Graphiques, Paris

Two Oriental Horsemen in Combat
c.1835
Pencil and sepia wash on paper
24.8 × 23.9 cm
On loan from the Musée du Louvre, Département des Arts Graphiques, Paris

Combat between the Giaour and the Pasha
1835
Oil on canvas
73 × 61 cm
On loan from the Musée du Petit Palais, Paris

Sketch for The Death of Sardanapalus
1826 –7
Pencil on paper
23.8 × 30.1 cm
On loan from the Musée du Louvre, Département des Arts Graphiques, Paris

Oil sketch for The Death of Sardanapalus
1826–7
Oil on canvas
81 × 100 cm
On loan from the Musée du Louvre, Département des Peintures, Paris

The Bride of Abydos
c.1849
Oil on panel
35 × 41 cm
On loan from King's College, Cambridge (Keynes Collection on loan to the Fitzwilliam Museum, Cambridge)

Odalisque
1825–8
Oil on canvas
37.8 × 46.4 cm
On loan from the Syndics of the Fitzwilliam Museum, Cambridge

Baron Dominique-Vivant Denon

Cleopatra's Needle
1798–9
Watercolour on paper
26 × 20.7 cm
On loan from the Board of Trustees of the Victoria and Albert Museum (Searight Collection), London

Théodule Devéria

Edfou: Facade of the Great Chamber of the Temple
1859
Albumen print from a paper negative
20.9 × 24 cm
On loan from La Bibliothèque du Louvre, Musée d'Orsay, Paris

Roger Fenton

The Valley of the Shadow of Death
1855
Salt print
27.1 × 36.4 cm
On loan from the Royal Photographic Society, Bath

Nubian Woman Carrying Water
c.1858
Albumen print
26.2 × 20.6 cm
On loan from the Royal Photographic Society, Bath

Louis Haghe after drawings by Gaspard Fossati

Aya Sofia, Constantinople, as recently restored by order of H.M. the Sultan Abdul Medjid, Plates 20–24
1852
Lithographs
56 × 46 cm
On loan from the National Library of Scotland, Edinburgh

Francis Frith

The Pyramids of Sakkarah from the North-East
1858
Albumen print
36.5 × 49.3 cm
Scottish National Portrait Gallery (Riddell Collection), Edinburgh

The Great Pyramid and The Great Sphinx
1858
Albumen print
38.5 × 49.5 cm
Scottish National Portrait Gallery (Riddell Collection), Edinburgh

Andrew Geddes

Sir William Allan
1815
Etching and drypoint
22.5 × 15.1 cm
National Gallery of Scotland, Department of Prints and Drawings, Edinburgh

Sir David Wilkie
1816
Oil on panel
66 × 48.2 cm
Scottish National Portrait Gallery, Edinburgh

Frederick Goodall

Early Morning in the Wilderness of Shur
1860
Oil on canvas
106.7 × 304.8 cm
On loan from Guildhall Art Gallery, Corporation of London

The Subsiding of the Nile
1873
Oil on canvas
76.2 × 152.4 cm
On loan from Guildhall Art Gallery, Corporation of London

Sir John Watson Gordon

John Frederick Lewis
c.1853
Oil on canvas
76.1 × 63.8 cm
On loan from the Royal Scottish Academy, Edinburgh

John B. Greene

Medinet Abu: Temple of Rameses III
1854
Calotype
23.2 × 29.9 cm
On loan from La Bibliothèque du Louvre, Musée d'Orsay, Paris

Medinet Abu: Temple of Rameses III
1854
Calotype
29.8 × 23.3 cm
On loan from La Bibliothèque du Louvre, Musée d'Orsay, Paris

Medinet Abu: Temple of Rameses III
1854
Calotype
23.5 × 29.7 cm
On loan from La Bibliothèque du Louvre, Musée d'Orsay, Paris

Medinet Abu: Temple of Rameses III
1854
Calotype
22.6 × 30.3 cm
On loan from La Bibliothèque du Louvre, Musée d'Orsay, Paris

Relief sculpture on a door jamb at Baie
1854
Calotype
33 × 22 cm
On loan from La Bibliothèque du Louvre, Musée d'Orsay, Paris

The Temple at Karnak: North Wall of the Hypostyle Hall
1854
Calotype
23.6 × 31 cm
On loan from La Bibliothèque du Louvre, Musée d'Orsay, Paris

John Hall after Gavin Hamilton

James Dawkins and Robert Wood, Esqrs. First Discovering Sight of Palmyra
1773 (after a painting of 1758)
Lithograph
44.5 × 52.7 cm
Scottish National Portrait Gallery, Edinburgh

Attributed to Robert Hay

Party Encamped in a Tomb in the Valley of the Kings
1827–34
Sepia wash on paper
37 × 48 cm
On loan from the British Library, London

Tomb Entrance with Animals and Birds in the Valley of the Kings
1827–34
Sepia wash on paper
32 × 24 cm
On loan from the British Library, London

William Hogarth

Procession in Hippodrome, Istanbul
1724
Engraving
26 × 35.1 cm
On loan from the Board of Trustees of the Victoria and Albert Museum (Searight Collection), London

William Holman Hunt

The Sphinx, Gizeh, Looking Towards the Pyramids of Sakkarah
1854
Watercolour on paper
25.4 × 35.5 cm
On loan from the Harris Museum and Art Gallery, Preston

Arab Reclining by a Stream
1854
Watercolour and touches of bodycolour on paper
25.4 × 35.3 cm
On loan from Sheffield City Art Galleries

The Plain of Rephaim from Mount Zion
1855
Watercolour on paper
35.3 × 50.5 cm
On loan from the Whitworth Art Gallery, University of Manchester

Jean-Auguste-Dominique Ingres

Odalisque with a Slave
1858
Graphite, gouache, sepia wash, pen and brown ink on paper
34.5 × 47.5 cm
On loan from the Musée du Louvre, Departément des Arts Graphiques, Paris

La Grande Odalisque
1825
Lithograph
16.3 × 22.6 cm
On loan from the Trustees of the British Museum, London

Edward William Lane

The Thousand and One Nights; or, The Arabian Nights' Entertainments, Vols. 1 & 2 (2nd edition).
Frontispiece designed by Owen Jones
1847
26 × 21 cm
On loan from the National Library of Scotland, Edinburgh

Notes and Views in Egypt and Nubia. Interior of Rock Temple
1826–7
Pencil on paper
25.3 × 17.5 cm
On loan from the British Library, London

Notes and Views in Egypt and Nubia. Head of the Northernmost Figure of Abu-Simbel
1826–7
Pencil on paper
25.3 × 17.2 cm
On loan from the British Library, London

Notes and Views in Egypt and Nubia. Court and Portico of the Great Temple at Kaleb Shah
1826–7
Pencil on paper
17.5 × 25.3 cm
On loan from the British Library, London

Notes and Views in Egypt and Nubia. Monument with Seated Figure
c.1826–7
Pencil on paper
25.2 × 17.4 cm
On loan from the British Library, London

Notes and Views in Egypt and Nubia. Grand Chamber of the Great Pyramid
1826–7
Pencil on paper
25.5 × 18 cm
On loan from the British Library, London

Notes and Views in Egypt and Nubia. Entrance to the Great Pyramid
1826–7
Pencil on paper
25.3 × 17.5 cm
On loan from the British Library, London

Notes and Views in Egypt and Nubia. View of the Pyramids
1826–7
Pencil and wash on paper
18 × 25.5 cm
On loan from the British Library, London

Notes and Views in Egypt and Nubia. Pyramids at Sunset
1826–7
Pencil on paper
17.6 × 25.3 cm
On loan from the British Library, London

Notes and Views in Egypt and Nubia. Costumes of the Ladies of Cairo
1826–7
Watercolour on paper
25.3 × 17.6 cm
On loan from the British Library, London

Richard James Lane

Edward William Lane
1829
Plaster
94 × 109.2 cm
On loan from the National Portrait Gallery, London

Robert Scott Lauder

David Roberts
1840
Oil on canvas
133 × 101.3 cm
Scottish National Portrait Gallery, Edinburgh

Edward Lear

The Pyramids Road, Gizeh
1873
Oil on canvas
53 × 104 cm
On loan from a Private Collection

A Distant View of Jerusalem
1858
Pen, ink and watercolour on paper
17.2 × 36.5 cm
On loan from a Private Collection

Philae at Sunset
1854
Pen, ink and watercolour on paper
17.3 × 24.6 cm
On loan from a Private Collection

Constantinople
1848
Pen, ink and watercolour on paper
19.5 × 32 cm
On loan from Bradford Art Galleries and Museum

The Falls of the Kalama, Albania
1857 (?)
Pen, ink and watercolour on paper
15.7 × 25.2 cm
On loan from a Private Collection

An Arab Encampment in the Sinai, near Gebal Serbal
Undated
Pen, ink and watercolour on paper
11.6 × 18 cm
On loan from a Private Collection

Frederick, Lord Leighton

Sir Richard Burton
1875
Oil on canvas
59.7 × 49.53 cm
On loan from the National Portrait Gallery, London

Richard and Isobel Burton's House in Damascus
1873
Oil on canvas
21.5 × 24 cm
On loan from Orleans House Gallery (on permanent loan from Southwark Libraries since 1969)

Old Damascus
1873–4
Oil on canvas
134 × 108 cm
On loan from a Private Collection

On the Nile
1868
Oil on canvas
27 × 41.6 cm
On loan from the Syndics of the Fitzwilliam Museum, Cambridge

Portion of the Interior of the Grand Mosque of Damascus
1873–5
Oil on canvas
158 × 122 cm
On loan from the Harris Museum and Art Gallery, Preston

John Frederick Lewis after Watteau

The Embarkation for the Island of Cythera
*c.*1827
Watercolour and gouache on paper
26.7 × 40 cm
On loan from the Royal Scottish Academy, Edinburgh

John Frederick Lewis after Delacroix

The Decapitation of the Doge Marino Faliero
*c.*1827
Watercolour and gouache on paper
23.8 × 18.8 cm
On loan from the Royal Scottish Academy, Edinburgh

John Frederick Lewis

The Harem
1850
Watercolour on paper
46 × 66.5 cm
On loan from the Board of Trustees of the Victoria and Albert Museum, London

The Mid-Day Meal
1875
Oil on canvas
87.6 × 115.6 cm
On loan from a Private Collection

A Turkish Woman
*c.*1841
Watercolour over black chalk on paper
35.8 × 25.3 cm
On loan from the Trustees of the British Museum, London

The Caged Doves
1864
Watercolour and bodycolour over pencil on paper
32.4 × 22.7 cm
On loan from the Syndics of the Fitzwilliam Museum, Cambridge

Armenian Girl
1841
Black chalk and watercolour, heightened with white on paper
50.4 × 36.9 cm
On loan from the Trustees of the British Museum, London

Indoor Gossip, Cairo: A Scene in a Harem
1873
Oil on panel
30.5 × 20.3 cm
On loan from the Whitworth Art Gallery, University of Manchester

School in Cairo
*c.*1853
Watercolour on paper
33.5 × 44.5 cm
On loan from the Board of Trustees of the Victoria and Albert Museum, London

The Arab Scribe, Cairo
1852
Watercolour on paper
46.3 × 61 cm
On loan from a Private Collection

The Street and Mosque of the Ghooreyah, Cairo
1876
Watercolour and oil on paper laid on panel
73.7 × 101 cm
On loan from the Forbes Magazine Collection, New York

Study for the Street and Mosque of the Ghooreyah, Cairo
*c.*1850
Watercolour, bodycolour and oil paint over pencil on thin buff paper
29 × 39.8 cm
On loan from Birmingham Museums and Art Gallery

Hagia Sophia, Constantinople: the Narthex
1840–1
Watercolour, bodycolour and black chalk on paper
30.1 × 38.9 cm
On loan from Birmingham Museums and Art Gallery

Courtyard of the Painter's House, Cairo
*c.*1851
Watercolour and bodycolour on five joined sheets
97.5 × 126 cm
On loan from Birmingham Museums and Art Gallery

A Camel
*c.*1851
Graphite on paper
26.3 × 39.1 cm
On loan from the Trustees of the British Museum, London

The Sheikh
1856
Oil on panel
43.2 × 30.5 cm
On loan from the Syndics of the Fitzwilliam Museum, Cambridge

Sellers of Antiquities, Thebes
c.1850
Black chalk with watercolour and bodycolour on buff paper
53.8 × 36.2 cm
On loan from the Syndics of the Fitzwilliam Museum, Cambridge

Hallicoo Mirza: Persian Exile in Constantinople
1841
Black chalk, watercolour and bodycolour on paper
36 × 48.1 cm
On loan from the Syndics of the Fitzwilliam Museum, Cambridge

Halt in the Desert
1855
Watercolour on paper
36.8 × 49.8 cm
On loan from the Board of Trustees of the Victoria and Albert Museum, London

Cataracts of the Nile at Aswan
c.1850
Pencil and watercolour on buff paper
36.5 × 52.6 cm
On loan from the Syndics of the Fitzwilliam Museum, Cambridge

Jean-Etienne Liotard

Man in Turkish Costume
c.1740–2
Black and red chalk with traces of wash on paper
17.2 × 18.7 cm
On loan from the Board of Trustees of the Victoria and Albert Museum, London

Philippe Jacques de Loutherbourg

A Sultana
Published 1777
Etching and stipple engraving
31 × 35 cm
On loan from the Board of Trustees of the Victoria and Albert Museum (Searight Collection), London

Sergeant James MacDonald

Ordnance Survey of the Peninsula of Sinai. Plates 6, 24, 30, 32, 34, 41
1869
Albumen prints
47 × 35 cm
On loan from the National Library of Scotland, Edinburgh

Patricia MacDonald

Seven photographs: Mirages I – VII, from 'Salt, Sand: Edge of Ocean, Edge of Dryness'
1992
Fujichrome prints
63.5 × 42.6 cm
On loan from the artist

Arthur Melville

Arab Interior
1881
Oil on canvas
95 × 72.8 cm
National Gallery of Scotland, Edinburgh

William James Müller

Opium Seller, Assiout
1838–9
Watercolour on paper
33.7 × 25.2 cm
On loan from the Trustees of the British Museum, London

Valley of the Tombs of the Queens
1839
Watercolour on paper
25.9 × 41.4 cm
On loan from the Trustees of the British Museum, London

Opium Seller
1838–9
Watercolour on paper
25.1 × 19 cm
On loan from the Trustees of the British Museum, London

Ruined Theatre at Xanthus
1843
Watercolour on paper
46.4 × 33.4 cm
On loan from a Private Collection

William Nicholson

Sir William Allan in Circassian Dress
1818
Oil on canvas
91.4 × 71.4 cm
Scottish National Portrait Gallery, Edinburgh

William Pars

Capital of Pilasters from the Temple of Apollo Didymaeus near Miletus
1765
Watercolour and gouache, pen and grey ink on paper
18 × 21 cm
On loan from the Trustees of the British Museum

Ruins of the Temple of Apollo Didymaeus from the North-East
1765
Watercolour and bodycolour on paper
30 × 47 cm
On loan from the Trustees of the British Museum, London

Matthew William Peters

Edward Wortley Montagu
c.1770
Oil on canvas
113.3 × 85.1 cm
On loan from the National Portrait Gallery, London

Henry W. Phillips

Lady Lucie Duff Gordon
1851
Oil on canvas
91.8 × 71.1 cm
On loan from the National Portrait Gallery, London

Thomas Phillips

Lord Byron
1835 (after a portrait of 1813)
Oil on canvas
76.5 × 63.8 cm
On loan from the National Portrait Gallery, London

Sir Edward Poynter

Israel in Egypt
1867
Oil on canvas
137.2 × 317.5 cm
On loan from Guildhall Art Gallery, Corporation of London

William Purser

View of Constantinople
1820–30s
Watercolour on paper
29.5 × 44.3 cm
On loan from the Board of Trustees of the Victoria and Albert Museum (Searight Collection), London

View of Constantinople
1820–30s
Watercolour on paper
30.2 × 45 cm
On loan from the Board of Trustees of the Victoria and Albert Museum (Searight Collection), London

David Roberts

Study for 'The Israelites leaving Egypt'
1827
Pen and tinted washes on paper
43.2 × 62.5 cm
On loan from the Trustees of the British Museum, London

Aaron delivering the Message of the Elders of Israel
c.1827
Watercolour and bodycolour on paper
22.6 × 31.5 cm
On loan from the Williamson Art Gallery and Museum, Birkenhead, Wirral

Tyre
1858
Oil on canvas
57.2 × 114.3 cm
On loan from Sheffield City Art Galleries

Interior of the Mosque of Metwalis
1839
Oil on canvas
29.2 × 39.4 cm
On loan from a Private Collection

The Holy Tree of Materia
1839
Watercolour on paper
33.7 × 23.5 cm
On loan from a Private Collection

Temple of Hermonthes, Upper Egypt
1843
Oil on panel
44 × 60 cm
On loan from a Private Collection

The Gateway of the Great Temple at Baalbec
1841
Oil on panel
75 × 62.2 cm
On loan from the Royal Academy of Arts, London

The Island of Philae, Nubia
1843
Oil on canvas
77.5 × 153.7 cm
On loan from a Private Collection

A General View of Cairo
1839
Pencil, watercolour and gouache on paper
52.7 × 300.4 cm
On loan from a Private Collection

Coffee Shop, Jaffa
*c.*1839
Watercolour, bodycolour and pencil on paper
19.9 × 28.6 cm
On loan from the Trustees of the British Museum, London

Temple at Wady Daboud
*c.*1839
Pencil and watercolour on paper
22.2 × 34.7 cm
On loan from the Board of Trustees of the Victoria and Albert Museum, London

Gulf of Aqaba
1839
Pencil and watercolour heightened with white on pale brown paper
20.4 × 34.7 cm
On loan from a Private Collection

Ancient Tartyris, Upper Egypt
1848
Pencil and watercolour on paper
48.2 × 34 cm
On loan from City of Aberdeen Art Gallery and Museums Collections

Temple of Philae
1838
Watercolour and bodycolour on grey paper
29.2 × 49.5 cm
On loan from a Private Collection

Gaza
1839
Watercolour on paper
34.9 × 49.9 cm
On loan from Glasgow Museums and Art Gallery

Colossi, Thebes
1838
Watercolour on grey-green paper
32 × 47.2 cm
On loan from Birmingham Museums and Art Gallery

Cairo Street Scene
1838
Pencil, watercolour and bodycolour on pale brown paper
46.8 × 30.4 cm
On loan from a Private Collection

James Robertson and Felice Beato

Ruins in Constantinople (?)
1850s
Albumen print from a glass negative
40 × 48 cm
On loan from the Musée d'Orsay, Paris

The Sultan Selim Fountain
1850s
Albumen print from a glass negative
40 × 48 cm
On loan from the Musée d'Orsay, Paris

Boats at The Suleymaniye
1850s
Albumen print from a glass negative
40 × 48 cm
On loan from the Musée d'Orsay, Paris

Hagia Sophia
1850s
Albumen print from a glass negative
40 × 48 cm
On loan from the Musée d'Orsay, Paris

The Suleymaniye
1850s
Albumen print from a glass negative
40 × 50 cm
On loan from the Musée d'Orsay, Paris

Base of the Obelisk
1850s
Albumen print from a glass negative
25.5 × 30 cm
On loan from the Musée d'Orsay, Paris

A Street in Constantinople
1850s
Albumen print from a glass negative
30.5 × 26.3 cm
On loan from the Musée d'Orsay, Paris

The Suleymaniye
1850s
Albumen print from a glass negative
30.5 × 24.4 cm
On loan from the Musée d'Orsay, Paris

Imperial Gateway to the Ancient Seraglio
1850s
Albumen print from a glass negative
25 × 27.5 cm
On loan from the Musée d'Orsay, Paris

Tombs of the Valide, Eyub
1850s
Albumen print from a glass negative
40 × 48 cm
On loan from the Musée d'Orsay, Paris

Figures at the Fountain of Sultan Ahmet III, Istanbul
1850s
Albumen print from a glass negative
30.3 × 26.4 cm
Scottish National Portrait Gallery, Edinburgh

Auguste Salzmann

Jerusalem: Arab Staircase
1854
Calotype
31.6 × 22.8 cm
On loan from the Musée d'Orsay, Paris (Gift of M. Robieu de Bry)

Jerusalem: Arab Fountain
1854
Calotype
32.5 × 23.3 cm
On loan from the Musée d'Orsay, Paris (Gift of M. Robieu de Bry)

Jerusalem: The Jaffa Gate
1854
Calotype
23.1 × 33.1 cm
On loan from the Musée d'Orsay, Paris (Gift of M. Robieu de Bry)

Jerusalem: Church of the Holy Sepulchre, West Door
1854
Calotype
32.6 × 23.3 cm
On loan from the Musée d'Orsay, Paris (Gift of M. Robieu de Bry)

Jerusalem: Tomb of the Judges, Detail
1854
Calotype
23.4 × 33 cm
On loan from the Musée d'Orsay, Paris (Gift of M. Robieu de Bry)

Jerusalem: The Valley of Hinnom, Detail of frieze
1854
Calotype
22.4 × 33.3 cm
On loan from the Musée d'Orsay, Paris (Gift of M. Robieu de Bry)

Jerusalem: The Walls of the Temple, Detail of the Golden Gate
1854
Calotype
32.7 × 22.8 cm
On loan from the Musée d'Orsay, Paris (Gift of M. Robieu de Bry)

Jerusalem: Judaic Tomb
1854
Calotype
23.2 × 33.1 cm
On loan from the Musée d'Orsay, Paris (Gift of M. Robieu de Bry)

Jerusalem: Arab Ornament
1854
Calotype
23.3 × 32.4 cm
On loan from the Musée d'Orsay, Paris (Gift of the Kodak-Pathé Foundation, Vincennes)

Jerusalem: The Walls of the Temple, Judaic moulding forming part of one of the Roman portals
1854
Calotype
32.8 × 22.5 cm
On loan from the Musée d'Orsay, Paris (Gift of M. Robieu de Bry)

Thomas Seddon

A Dromedary and an Arab in the City of the Dead, Cairo, with the Tomb of the Sultan El-Barook in the Background
1854
Oil on canvas
27.5 × 36 cm
On loan from Andrew McIntosh Patrick

Jerusalem and the Valley of Jehoshaphat from the Hill of Evil Counsel
1854–5
Oil on canvas
67.3 × 83.2 cm
On loan from the Trustees of the Tate Gallery, London

Arabs at Prayer in the Desert
c.1855
Oil on canvas (unfinished)
50 × 90 cm
On loan from the Forbes Magazine Collection, New York

Lieutenant Richard Burton in Arab Dress
1853
Watercolour on paper
28.5 × 20 cm
On loan from Andrew McIntosh Patrick

Félix Teynard

Tomb of Amenemhat at Beni Hasan from 'Egypt and Nubia, Sites and Monuments'
1851–2
Salt print from a paper negative
24.6 × 31 cm
On loan from La Bibliothèque du Louvre, Musée d'Orsay, Paris

Medinet Abu, Thebes: Structures at the back of the 2nd Court of the North-West Gallery from 'Egypt and Nubia, Sites and Monuments'
1851–2
Salt print from a paper negative
30.5 × 24.5 cm
On loan from La Bibliothèque du Louvre, Musée d'Orsay, Paris

Medinet Abu, Thebes: Structures at the back of the 2nd Court of the South-West Gallery from 'Egypt and Nubia, Sites and Monuments'
1851–2
Salt print from a paper negative
30.7 × 25.2 cm
On loan from La Bibliothèque du Louvre, Musée d'Orsay, Paris

Esna: Structure covered with sand, architrave, column shafts and capitals from 'Egypt and Nubia, Sites and Monuments'
1851–2
Salt print from a paper negative
23.9 × 30.6 cm
On loan from La Bibliothèque du Louvre, Musée d'Orsay, Paris

Arab Cemetery at Aswan: Funerary inscriptions from 'Egypt and Nubia, Sites and Monuments'
1851–2
Salt print from a paper negative
29.3 × 30.9 cm
On loan from La Bibliothèque du Louvre, Musée d'Orsay, Paris

Philae: French inscription carved on the eastern embrasure at Point H from 'Egypt and Nubia, Sites and Monuments'
1851–2
Salt print from a paper negative
24 × 31 cm
On loan from La Bibliothèque du Louvre, Musée d'Orsay, Paris

Ed-Derr: Monument carved into the bedrock; pillars and carved sculptures at the left side from 'Egypt and Nubia, Sites and Monuments'
1851–2
Salt print from a paper negative
23.8 × 30.8 cm
On loan from La Bibliothèque du Louvre, Musée d'Orsay, Paris

Abu Simbel: Speos – Colossal Statues Seen at Three-Quarters View from 'Egypt and Nubia, Sites and Monuments'
1851–2
Salt print from a paper negtaive
30.4 × 24.9 cm
On loan from La Bibliothèque du Louvre, Musée d'Orsay, Paris

Abu Simbel: Large Speos – Colossal Statues Seen from the Front from 'Egypt and Nubia, Sites and Monuments'
1851–2
Salt print from a paper negative
24.3 × 31 cm
On loan from La Bibliothèque du Louvre, Musée d'Orsay, Paris

Joseph Mallord William Turner

Babylon
1830s
Watercolour on paper
14.4 × 21 cm
On loan from the Board of Trustees of the Victoria and Albert Museum, London

Hagia Sophia, Constantinople
1830s
Watercolour on paper
16.5 × 24 cm
On loan from the Board of Trustees of the Victoria and Albert Museum, London

Unknown, Greek School

Hippodrome, Constantinople
1820s
Watercolour on paper
41.5 × 63 cm
On loan from the Board of Trustees of the Victoria and Albert Museum (Searight Collection), London

Street in Pera
1820s
Watercolour on paper
40.5 × 60.3 cm
On loan from the Board of Trustees of the Victoria and Albert Museum (Searight Collection), London

Kaymakam receiving Europeans
1820s
Watercolour on paper
21.3 × 33.5 cm
On loan from the Board of Trustees of the Victoria and Albert Museum (Searight Collection), London

Unknown

View of a Gateway in Constantinople
Undated
Pencil and watercolour on paper
35.6 × 45.7 cm
On loan from a Private Collection

Robert Hay and members of his expedition to Egypt
c.1833
Pencil on paper
37 × 48 cm
On loan from the British Library, London

Attributed to Jean-Baptiste Vanmour

Lady Mary Wortley Montagu
c.1716
Oil on canvas
68.6 × 90.2 cm
On loan from the National Portrait Gallery, London

Lewis Vuilliamy

Fountain of Tophane, Istanbul
c.1818
Pencil on paper
26.6 × 40.8 cm
On loan from the Board of Trustees of the Victoria and Albert Museum, London (Searight Collection)

Jean-Antoine Watteau

Fêtes Vénitiennes
1718–19
Oil on canvas
55.9 × 45.7 cm
National Gallery of Scotland, Edinburgh

Figure in Turkish Costume
Undated
Black and red chalk on paper
20.2 × 10.1 cm
On loan from the Trustees of the British Museum, London

Sir David Wilkie

Sultan of Turkey – His Imperial Majesty the Sultan Abdul Medgid
Published 1843
Lithograph
38 × 29.5 cm
On loan from the Board of Trustees of the Victoria and Albert Museum (Searight Collection), London

Sketches in Turkey, Syria and Egypt. Plate 14, The Dragoman of Mr Moore, English Consul at Beyrout
Published 1843
Lithograph
55 × 39 cm
On loan from the National Library of Scotland, Edinburgh

Sketches in Turkey, Syria and Egypt. Plate 26, Hebrew Women Reading the Scriptures at Jerusalem
Published 1843
Lithograph
55 × 39 cm
On loan from the National Library of Scotland, Edinburgh

Sketches in Turkey, Syria and Egypt. Plate 16, Camels – Sketches at Smyrna
Published 1843
Lithograph
55 × 39 cm
On loan from the National Library of Scotland, Edinburgh

Study for The Turkish Letter-Writer
1840
Black chalk and watercolour, heightened with white chalk on paper
37.1 × 29.6 cm
On loan from the Visitors of the Ashmolean Museum, Oxford

The Dragoman of Mr Allison at Pera
1840
Black and red chalks, and oil pigments and bodycolours, on buff or brown paper
44.3 × 27.2 cm
On loan from the Visitors of the Ashmolean Museum, Oxford

The Tartar Messenger Narrating the News of the Victory of St Jean d'Acre
1840
Oil on panel
68.6 × 53.3 cm
On loan from a Private Collection

Group of Men. Sketch for The Tartar Messenger
1840
Pencil, pen and brown ink on paper
37 × 24.5 cm
On loan from the Board of Trustees of the Victoria and Albert Museum (Searight Collection), London

Muhammad Ali
1841
Oil on board
61 × 50.8 cm
On loan from the Trustees of the Tate Gallery, London

Portrait of Sotiri, Dragoman of Mr Colquhoun
1840
Watercolour, bodycolour and oil, over pencil, on buff paper
47.5 × 32.8 cm
On loan from the Visitors of the Ashmolean Museum, Oxford

A Persian Prince (previously known as 'A Turk Taking Refreshment')
1840
Chalk, wash and watercolour on paper
46 × 31.6 cm
On loan from City of Aberdeen Art Gallery and Museums Collections

An Arab Muleteer
1841
Black and red chalk with watercolour and bodycolour on buff paper
54.6 × 38.3 cm
National Gallery of Scotland, Department of Prints and Drawings, Edinburgh

Eastern Woman with a Baby
1840–41
Black chalk and watercolour heightened with white on paper
28.8 × 24 cm
National Gallery of Scotland, Department of Prints and Drawings, Edinburgh

The Infant Daughter of Admiral Walker in Turkish Dress
1840
Pencil, black chalk and watercolour with white highlights on paper
39.5 × 28.6 cm
On loan from the Syndics of the Fitzwilliam Museum, Cambridge

Mrs Moore
1841
Pencil, black and red chalk, watercolour, heightened with white on paper
45.4 × 33 cm
On loan from the Syndics of the Fitzwilliam Museum, Cambridge

Madame Josephina, Landlady of the Hotel, Constantinople
1840
Pencil, chalk, watercolour and bodycolour on paper
47.2 × 33.1 cm
On loan from the Courtauld Institute Galleries (Spooner Collection), London